C0-AVA-216

5400
————
2/0

THE PROTESTANT CREDO

BOOKS BY VERGILIUS FERM

The Crisis in American Lutheran Theology (1927)

What is Lutheranism? (1930), Editor

Contemporary American Theology, Theological Autobiographies, Volume I (1932), Editor

Contemporary American Theology, Theological Autobiographies, Volume II (1933), Editor

First Adventures in Philosophy (1936)

Religion in Transition (1937), Editor

First Chapters in Religious Philosophy (1937)

An Encyclopedia of Religion (1945), Editor

Religion in the Twentieth Century (1948), Editor

What Can We Believe? (1948)

Forgotten Religions (1950), Editor

A History of Philosophical Systems (1950), Editor

A Protestant Dictionary (1951)

The American Church (1953), Editor

Puritan Sage, The Collected Writings of Jonathan Edwards (1953), Editor

The Protestant Credo (1953), Editor

THE PROTESTANT CREDO

Edited By

VERGILIUS FERM

*Compton Professor and Head of the Department of Philosophy
in The College of Wooster*

PHILOSOPHICAL LIBRARY
New York

284
P946

123941

Copyright, 1953, By
THE PHILOSOPHICAL LIBRARY, Inc.
15 East 40th Street, New York, N. Y.

PRINTED IN THE UNITED STATES OF AMERICA

TABLE OF CONTENTS

List of Contributors

Gaius Glenn Atkins

John Coleman Bennett

Francis William Buckler

Morton Scott Enslin

Vergilius Ferm

Francis John McConnell

John Thomas McNeill

Conrad Henry Moehlman

Floyd H. Ross

Henry Nelson Wieman

Acknowledgments

THE EDITOR EXPRESSES HIS THANKS

To his publisher, Dagobert D. Runes, Ph.D., president of The Philosophical Library, for the germinal ideas which went into the mutual planning of this volume and for the unfailing support in the work of its execution—

And to the Trustees of The College of Wooster for the privilege of a second sabbatical leave in order to pursue this and other literary projects—

But especially to the contributors to this volume whose cooperative interest has made pleasant the task.

PREFACE

WHAT we have sought to do in this volume is to state the Protestant faith and its essentials. We have had primarily in mind people such as Mr. Brown and Mrs. Johnson and Miss McClarren and young Joe Doe, intelligent Protestants who sit in church pews—it may not be regularly—calling themselves Protestant but not too sure why. We are thinking especially of those laymen who are alert and intelligent and for whom the Protestant faith would be more realistic if they could understand it a little better in terms of the broad sweep of its historical character and of its contemporary significance. We have had also in mind, in the case of some of the essays, professional people such as ministers and teachers whose eyes are ever on the alert for fresh insights and interpretations of Protestantism as a significant religious pattern of thought in the contemporary world.

Catholics know the value of such books for their people. Rightly they publish their positions by paid advertisements in nationally circulated papers and magazines and their priests write accounts stating plainly and succinctly the characteristic features of their faith and its reasonableness. Protestants have done this in a more separated way: a denomination issues books on its own denominational views and polity. But people are less interested today in denominations. They want to know more about the bigger things, the ideas they are supposed to have in common with others who together claim a similar rootage and tradition. Protestants may well try to state their positions as Protestants, not as Lutherans or Methodists or Baptists or Congregationalists. This book is written and published to serve toward that end—a collective cross-section portrayal of the Protestant Credo in the light of to-day's world.

Readers will find here a plurality of views and may be somewhat disturbed by the variety. If it is absolute homogeneity they look for in the Protestant faith they have come into the wrong place. It is Catholicism that has tried (although not altogether successfully) to make out a clean-cut creed and a clean-cut program. It is the very genius of Protestantism to have under the banner of its name the imprint of diversity since Protestantism is a movement coming from people who are inherently individuals and not puppets under one system or authority. The many denominations under the term Protestant are no accidents of history. They are part and parcel of the result of liberated consciences, of the freedom of people to assert their own experiences and expressions of the Divine, of a fundamental distrust of any form of tyranny of thought which would crush the inner soul.

This book will not appeal to those who follow the radical cults whose genius consists in the enthusiastic following of some self-anointed enthusiastic religious leader with special information and undisciplined interpretations. They have their place and there will always be such followers of such leaders. It is to the faithful in the Protestant heritage to whom this book is addressed whose outlook is not as clear as it might be in terms of the broad issues of their form of Christianity. It is also to those who once were of the fold but who have somehow lost touch and carry a pinch of regret.

Contributors to this book are liberal Protestants—liberal but not radical. Each one knows the history of the churches and their doctrines full well. Witness to this fact is given in the editorial biographies accompanying each essay.

To organize such a volume as this, an editor must make some concrete suggestions to the company who joins the venture. Some of these suggestions were as follows: With a Protestant layman in mind, what makes a person a Protestant, other than being born one? What ideas are basic to Protestantism? What, for example, may be affirmed about God, the church, the sacraments, Jesus Christ, the Scriptures, attitude toward others of other faith-persuasions, efforts towards unity, the good life (*summum bonum*), life after death, prayer, evil, sin, salvation, grace, the Divine concern, the kingdom of God, the ministry and the laymen, social implications of the faith, questions of organization or polity. Leaving dissonances in the background, what may be said to constitute basic agreements and the common direction among Protestants? Such were some of the questions, each writer free to make his own selection and emphasis of topics and, if he chose, his own generalizations.

It was directed that each one give a testimony not so much as a professional student (though, of course, professional interests are never overcome) but rather as a person who has, by his years of reflection, come to his own warm conclusions. This book, in other words, claims not scholarly self-consciousness on the part of the writers; rather, it is a collection of essays of the kind that writers might set down informally without an undue awareness that their statements wear the air of comprehensiveness or finality. Each contributor has been made to feel that, had the assignment come earlier or later, the testimony might well have been handled differently. Professionalism thus has given way to that of approaching face-to-face talking. Naturally, then, each writer has felt free to tap his particular area of intensive interest in the light of his own particular reflections and concern.

A figure of speech may summarize the function of the volume: It is like a roof held up by ten pillars, none of which duplicates the other (in the spirit of Protestantism) but all of which have something intrinsically alike sharing in the support of some common structure.

VERGILIUS FERM

The College of Wooster

MY PROTESTANT HERITAGE

By

GAIUS GLENN ATKINS

GAIUS GLENN ATKINS

Those whose memories go back to the earlier decades of this century will remember the name of Gaius Glenn Atkins as one of the six or eight in the circle of America's greatest preachers. His notable ministry in the First Congregational Church of Detroit, 1906-1910, and again 1917-1927, and at Central Church in Providence, Rhode Island, 1910-1917, not to mention other pulpits including those on American campuses from which his voice was heard, marked him as a unique figure among those in the sacred profession. His mind always has seemed to be renewed with freshness of interpretation of religious themes due in large part to the wide horizons of his thought and reading in far flung fields which were to him never remote from religious implications. He was a preacher's preacher. At Auburn Theological Seminary he taught the art of preaching and is now, since 1937, its professor emeritus. A lover of books he taught others a similar love. A social thinker he has never ceased to be an optimist for the realization in fact of a kingdom of God on the earth—even amidst the pessimisms that followed in the wake of wars, social revolutions and economic depressions. His books reveal the depth of his own mind and understanding: such, among so many, as "Pilgrims of the Lonely Road" (1913); "The Undiscovered Country" (1922); "The Making of the Christian Mind" (1928); "Resources for Living" (1938); besides the well-known and widely read study of religious isms entitled "Modern Religious Cults and Movements" (1923). He is the kind of writer who expresses himself from the overflow. When his thoughts focus upon a subject he sees beyond it wider areas and we are not surprised to find that his interpretation of Protestantism has the vista of catholicism and ecumenicity which breaks through the fences of conventional boundaries.

Editor

MY PROTESTANT HERITAGE

Gaius Glenn Atkins

Dr. Ferm's suggestions of what the contributors to this book may write are almost too generous. No contributor could follow them all. Indeed, any one of them would itself ask for a book. The alcoves of great libraries have shelves of books on almost any one of his suggested subjects. Each contributor will, therefore, I suspect, take his own line in one way or another. One can hope with good reason that the total result will be inclusive and helpful. The need for definition and clarification of the Protestant position is very urgent. I, myself, have read and thought and preached and taught within the areas of Protestantism for years, though never as a controversialist and for the most part without thinking of myself as a Protestant at all; only as a seeker for the full meaning and power of the Way and the Truth and the Life of Jesus Christ; a very great deal of this has been as natural to me as breathing and I have never needed to give it specific control, more than I needed to be self-conscious about my breathing.

> I like a church, I like a cowl;
> I love a prophet of the soul,
> And on my heart monastic aisles
> Fall like sweet strains or pensive smiles,
> Yet not for all his faith can see
> What I that cowléd churchman be.

I think myself, as most of us do, that Protestantism was unfortunately named; almost by an historical accident. The name dates from the Diet of Speyer in 1529 when a workable adjustment between the followers of Luther and the old Church was sought. Lutheranism, the Diet decided, should be tolerated in German lands where it could not be suppressed.

[3]

THE PROTESTANT CREDO

There the Catholic minorities were to enjoy religious liberty. But no religious liberty would be granted Lutheran minorities in Catholic lands. Naturally the evangelicals protested,— what else could they do?—this invidious arrangement. It made of religious liberty only a one-way street. The protestants affirmed that "they must protest and testify before God that they could do nothing contrary to His word". "The emphasis," says Bainton, (*The Reformation in the 16th Century*), "was less on protest, than on witness." One may justly be proud of a fellowship so christened.

We still do our share of protesting, naturally, since in our kind of world there are, and always have been, a plentitude of things against which to protest and, to be specific, the Roman Catholic Church does its share. Actually Protestantism is positive, creative, affirmative. There are suggestive parallels between the Diet of Speyer, from which the name Protestantism dates, and the group which framed and proclaimed the American Declaration of Independence. There is protest enough in that—complaints made precise. But actually the issue in both cases was positive and creative.

Protestantism has created churches, creeds, theologies, literatures, civilization, generations of good men and women and its own saints, though they may not have been calendared. And it has done all this in its own ways. Without those ways, a very great deal which is an invaluable part of our own American life would apparently never have existed at all, for we have trusted the free course of the questing soul and the inquiring mind and sought for them the guidance of God.

* * *

Oliver Wendell Holmes said, I seem to remember, "that one's education should begin at least with his grandfather." I am not now able to verify that recollection and a thoughtful friend searched for the quotation in Holmes' writings and did not find it. But I stand by it nevertheless, for it is true even if Holmes never said it. My only remark is that he did not go back far enough.

[4]

MY PROTESTANT HERITAGE

I am a Protestant through ancestral generations which go back to Amsterdam in Holland and, I suspect, to the hills and vales of Wales. Inherited faiths and attitudes drawn through centuries from now untraceable confluent sources have combined to make me what I am; which is no important matter save that most Protestants are like that and most Roman Catholics are like that also. One of our most important challenges is to understand ourselves which is generally the first condition of understanding other people.

History, since history began, is full of vanished alternatives. "If and if and if", historians say, this had not happened, or this other way had been chosen, issues of vast significance might have been channeled otherwise than they were and history itself would need to be rewritten, though no one would know how. Again and again, apparently, the deflecting forces seemed of so little consequence that no one could foresee what would happen; as though the wind should determine on which side of a continental divide a raindrop should fall and into what ocean it would eventually be carried. Such speculations are fascinating. But I believe that in their ends and issues great historical movements are directed by a confluence of forces, often in long and unsuspected action, before they break through the forms or barriers which seem to restrain them. And I believe that the great issues of history are not accidents.

There are thus alternatives to the lines which church history began to take at the beginning of the 16th century. Erasmus, for example, and the men of the new learning, hoped for a gradual bettering of conditions which were becoming intolerable through the illumination of the leaders of the Latin Catholic Church with consequent readjustment and reform from within. If Martin Luther had never nailed his theses to the church doors at Wittenberg, he himself unwitting of how far his hammer strokes would reach, or what would fall before them, the history of the last three centuries might have been strangely different. But this is only one more vanished alternative. "Things," said Bishop Butler, "are what they are, and the consequences of them will be what they will be."

The travail of the Reformation was a long and costly labor, but the ends have justified it, both for the old Church and the new Churches. The Christian order may have lost unity of form and administration, but it has gained an immeasurable wealth in content and power.

We Protestants have not lost our birthrights in twenty centuries of Christian history. They are still our heritage, for an "heritage", the dictionary says, is far more noble and elevated than an "inheritance". It has intellectual, moral and spiritual dimensions. As a Protestant I claim as part of my religious heritage, all that the great Christian orders have been. I claim as a birthright the Saints, Apostles, Prophets and Martyrs. The golden-mouthed preachers are still mine. The great creeds, and incidentally the great controversies, Abailard and St. Bernard are ours; the *Te Deum* and "Jerusalem the Golden", the monks who saved for us literatures which otherwise would have been hopelessly lost, the *Imitation of Christ* and the windows of Chartre and the Sainte Chapelle, the sculptured front of Armiens, and the towers of Notre Dame, the liturgies and pageantry of the Latin Church—are all ours. But what is more; without the Reformation, we would never have had the freedom to accept and evaluate these heritages without any compulsion save their own values and integrities, as all great things are meant to be possessed.

It is thus, I repeat, that we share together, speaking inclusively, the Christian faith and the sovereign Christian inheritances. The Reformation, fundamentally, involved the seat of authority, rather than the veracity of creed. Great communions which belong to the Protestant fellowship use the Nicene and the Athanasian Creeds and the Apostles', the oldest of them all. The Communions which separated from Rome continued the essential Christian faith. I do not believe that the emphases which leaders like Luther, or John Calvin, put upon their own doctrinal positions, controversial as they may have been, greatly affected the real Christian faith and loyalties of the continuing generation. But something was changed for all that. There was a definite release and access of freedom. The liberty of the Christian man, for which St. Paul lived, taught and died, was released and reaffirmed to become an incalculable force. Even the clearest vision of the Reformers, who saw the far issue of this only in part, recognized the need of a controlling authority and on the bases of their own interpretation of the New Testament created their own authoritative systems. But for all that, even the most authoritarian of the historic Protestant communion at least took the liberty to replace the authority of Rome with the authorities of their own ecclesiastical orders.

Liberty is always a trust and a challenge. St. Paul knew that. And all who love and seek liberty and desire the full fruition of it, in mind and spirit, have known that ever since. It is not easy to be free: our Protestant inheritances in churches, polities and creed have testified to that, both happily and unhappily, and, in the ultimate issues, creatively. There were excesses in the exercise of such liberty and the issue was undue division supported by immaterial contention. We are beginning to heal the wounds of our divisions, to make whole again what has been splintered. Really vast unifying forces are now in action which have already forecast the working union of all non-Roman Catholic churches. There are still unbridged gaps and together they present an almost unbelievably wide front. But they begin to move on together.

*　　*　　*

My own Protestant Credo, though I would not particularly underscore Protestant, since it is just the way my mind and spirit naturally work, includes many articles. I would put rather high up on the list the influence and importance of Christian laymen and women in Protestant Churches. I do not for a moment doubt that Roman Catholic polity is influenced, though in crucial matters very slowly, by the opinions of

Catholic laymen. The parts that laymen take, or may take, in Protestant communions differ widely. But the laymen and women are there. They are responsible and they are free enough to make themselves count. Every layman who reads this knows that. He may say of his faith and his loyalties what St. Paul told the Roman Captain "But I was free born", never forgetting the price his freedom cost and cherishing it as a sacred trust. It is, to repeat, not easy to be free ever— especially when old orders are breaking up and new orders have not yet taken either final or supporting form.

Fifty years ago Matthew Arnold who felt very deeply the dissolution of inherited faith and authorities foresaw and foretold that many, not equal to the strain, would seek centralized authority which allowed no appeal from itself both in church and state, although Arnold himself did not for a moment anticipate the forms authoritarianism would take in the governments of states. What he foresaw has happened. But it is not the right way out. It is an escape, the issues of which in the break up of long established national and social orders, have been and are what the newspapers headline. It is not easy to be free nobly, loyally and obediently free; but even the partial achievement of it is the greatest accomplishment of which we are capable.

I find in Protestantism a virtue which has come up for much criticism. We are never alike. We all share the same fundamental religious needs but we are anything but alike in the ways in which we seek to meet them and think they can be met. The varieties of Protestantism have been carried to excess, but there must be room, taking the human spirit in its entirety, for the silence of the Friend wih his "concern" for God's will and the liturgies of the High Churches; room for the creeds which make faith voluminously precise; and the creeds which ask no more of Christian discipleship than Jesus Himself asked "Deny yourself, take up your Cross and follow me."

Because I believe in the freedom of the mind, in education,

scientific exploration and social wisdom, I find the Protestant attitude congenial, allowing for all qualifications. We have no *Index* of forbidden books, though there are books enough which no one of decent taste would care to read. I do not believe that the restless and ranging movements of the human mind, though always requiring discipline, should be subjected to any ecclesiastical control. In the long run, truth will verify itself and assert its own authority. We so conceive the free and vast movements of the spirit of God that we do not believe any Church is the channel through which all thought should flow.

I believe it has an irritating power to overflow its banks and to fertilize and make beautiful and fruitful every right dimension of life. I believe that religion should inform and influence every aspect of soundly intellectual education, but it should not be made subject to the ends of any ecclesiastical authority. I believe that the methods and spirit of Protestantism serve naturally and without strain the processes of democracy. The historic relations between the Reformed faiths and cultures and democracy are no accident. They drain from deep and unifying sources one and indivisible. The whys and wherefores of this are beyond the space limits of this article, but again and again civic freedom has been nurtured in religious freedom. I do not believe that democracy will survive strains and tensions without a religious basis, but that basis must itself be free on the highest levels of intellectual, moral and spiritual freedom.

*   *   *

The relation between Protestantism and free and representative governments is in itself a historic study of very great magnitude in which naturally there is room for marked differences of opinion. Allowing for all the causes of the Reformation, it nevertheless required in its beginning great courage and independency. And it required great courage and independency to carry it through. It is never easy to leave the shelters and assurances of long established patterns for the hazardous and the untried. It was inevitable that the liberty to do just that should become crucial and be maintained, sometimes at terrible cost, by the new religious orders. Even as in England where to begin with, the inherited Catholic order was least changed, the Constitution of the Church had eventually to become much modified.

John Calvin wrought out, quite literally, a constitution *de novo* for his followers except that he believed himself to be recreating the Church of the Apostles, and the men who made a church were very likely to set out in the end to make a state, since making a church and making a state were one and indivisible in their nature. And those who did it had in some measure little or great to be free and at whatever cost to affirm and maintain their freedom. The result has been a profound and sustaining affinity between the Protestant way and democratic and representative government.

I do not say that here in America the Roman Catholic order is alien, in secular practice, to democratic and representative government, but the very theory and structure of the final authority of the church in all political and secular affairs, is, to put it plainly, an indigestible element in a democracy or republic—a pressure to use the mechanisms of free government to further the ends of the church is almost inevitable. The release of the full excommunicating power of the church against civil authority is now extremely unlikely to be used, but the theory of the right to use it has not been surrendered.

* * *

Nothing, I suppose, would be gained by carrying an article like this into acutely controversial regions. There are innumerable things possible to believe; for many, many people do believe what to others may seem impossible. But Protestantism on the whole does not burden faith with marginal things. I can understand the place of saints in Roman Catholic worship. They help bridge for worshippers the spaces between human experience and the sovereignties of God. Some of them came up out of great tribulation. They can, therefore, sympathize and understand others in tribulation and, so to speak, forward prayers which might not reach the Divine presence. But their worship is not necessarily included in a Protestant Credo,—nor much else which does not need to be named here. Faith may therefore be less burdened and able to focus upon the essential. I appreciate the pageantry of Roman Catholic worship to which Protestantism in its extreme liturgical forms approximates, or even over-approximates. But Protestant worship is for the most part more simple. It still carries the fundamental expression of confession, prayer and praise. But, at our best, we achieve a fellowship of worship in which participation is less patterned, a worship in spirit and in truth. Protestantism cannot well be understood without its hymn books, its hymns and their histories. It has a wealth and range of hymnology, not all, of course, its own. Many of its hymns belong to the historic Christian order and may be shared or appropriated by any communion. But there is a treasured wealth of hymns which is the enduring expression of a free faith, a devout spirit and a sense of the unfailing and unmediated nearness of God.

Protestantism began, and has since continued, in a fellowship of songs which are part of our childhood memory and are associated with our most tender and treasured experience. Protestantism rebaptized worship in living languages and made it possible for the worshipper to repeat the experience of the Day of Pentecost and hear each one in his own tongue.

* * *

The Protestant communions, of course, have different conceptions of the Christian ministry and difficult questions about ordination divide our fellowships, unhappily, and make complete unity troublesome and even divide us at the Table of Our Lord. Here, I think, the sovereign divisions of Protestantism come to a head. But, in the main, the Protestant ministry is conceived as a normal part of our intricate human relationships. For the most part, I say this with qualifications. Protestant ministers do not conceive themselves as separated in ordination by an impassable gulf between themselves and their congregation. Protestantism, for the most part, has affirmed the priesthood of all believers, a phrase needing much clarification; but it does mean that God is near to us and directly accessible to our individual approaches. This lends a dignity and worth to the Christian life which cannot easily be put into words, but which we may feel in our inner devotional lives.

We ordain our ministers and we do not agree in our conceptions of ordination, nor upon the authorities which are able to confer it. In the Communions which stress the crucial importance of the episcopate, ordination being given through the proper channels is held to continue and bestow a particular spiritual power and authority not easy to put in words, but held to validate those ordained through their relation by historic succession with the ministry of Jesus and His Apostles. For other Communions ordination establishes a peculiar ecclesiastical and legal status. With others ordination means the recognition and proper establishment of those called to be ministers of the Gospel. But, in general, ordination is the recognition of the goodness and wisdom and special calling of those ordained symbolized by the laying on of hands.

With the exception of the Friends who seek no symbol for the outward and evident signs of an inward and spiritual grace all Protestant Communions agree at least in the reality and importance of the two sacraments, baptism and the Lord's Supper.

It is one of the offices of Protestantism that it meets the religious needs of all sorts of conditions of people along a wide front and there are consequently different conceptions of the sacraments, particularly the Lord's Supper. But we do not burden the bread and the wine upon the communion table or altar with conceptions of change and real presences from which in their extreme form the Reformation was an emancipation. Our Communions vary in their liturgies and methods of administration but we are conscious of our Master's presence and share again His sacrifice in the cup and the broken bread.

For the most part we do not believe that Jesus Christ bequeathed to us His Church in details of organization, succession and authority. We believe that He left His disciples and all those who have followed them a free and creative spirit to be exercised through subsequent generations and under changing conditions, and that He was more concerned for the extension of the Christian way and the growth of Christians in grace and goodness than in forms of ecclesiastical ordination and gradations of ecclesiastical authority.

We believe, therefore, that there is a liberty of choice in church forms, organizations and disciplines to meet the range of our various minds and needs. The Christian church proclaims the Gospel of salvation but no church possesses it as a monopoly, for the love of God is broader than the measure of mankind. Jesus never meant by any record left us of His words and His mind to make the Kingdom of God He proclaimed only another name for any Church. It is too vast and more inclusive than that. New Testament scholars are not agreed about what Jesus meant by the Kingdom of Heaven or of God, nor when it was to come; but we do believe there are possible ways of living together here and now, near or far, and doing our work in ways in which God's will, as Jesus taught us to pray, might be done on earth, as it is in heaven. We believe that Jesus' teachings are a guide-book to that way. We do not believe any church right enough, or big enough, to be the whole Kingdom of God. We believe that all churches should seek and serve it and so from generation to generation instruct and inspire their leaders.

Protestantism has no monopoly of what is loosely called the Social Gospel though I think it may claim a priority in its development and application. The social proclamations of the head of the Catholic church have been inclusive and far-seeing, but, for all that, I believe there is a grass-root relation between Protestantism and efforts for some here-and-now realization of the realm of God amongst us. For one thing, as I have said, we do not identify the Kingdom of God and the Church which gives Protestantism a much wider front to work, along with freer and more elastic methods. The ruling motivations of the Social Gospel and the enthralling ideal of a Divine Order amongst us, for which when I began my ministry the morning stars sang together, is now apparently dated; but I have never surrendered it and I believe the Christian churches have a mandate to seek and to seek better and more Christian orders in every relationship of life. This they can accomplish if they will seek it freely and creatively, at whatever cost, and find power in doing it. It does not grow more easy. It grows more difficult and complicated. We have no choice but to go on or to see the collapse of all our cherished orders. And I, as a Protestant, do not feel that an untroubled life in heaven can wholly compensate for not having tried to realize the Kingdom of Heaven here on earth. I think the recollections of that failure might cloud a little the heavenly felicities.

These last three or four paragraphs deserve an expansion in comment and illustration, not here possible. When one considers the epochal significance of books which have been, or still are, on lists of books forbidden to the faithful, I cannot help believing that if the free movements of the mind are to be subject to ecclesiastical control, irreparable harm would be done to free inquiry. Ecclesiastical authority has always had a way of seeking to subordinate too much to its own causes and interests, and incidentally has done great harm to those very causes and interests.

There are unescapable processes of trial and error in every quest. They are the conditions, sometimes costly, of any advance in any field. Protestantism has by no means entirely escaped them, but its trust in the free movements of the inquiring mind have been justified by every test. I count the liberty to think with no constraint save an honest devotion to truth and right, as they are discoverable, an invaluable part of the Protestant heritage and a service even to the ecclesiastical authorities which seem to deny that liberty. The proof of that, not always recognized and acknowledged, is that the Catholic Church has grown and prospered and revealed powers of self-correction here in America, as nowhere else.

Historic Protestantism has faults and failures enough to confess, though it has no monopoly of fault and failure. But we believe that it has, by the Grace of God, continually demonstrated a healing and saving power of self-correction and that it is teachable and learns from experience.

*   *   *

Protestantism treasures a long and shining list of those who have paid the last full measure of devotion for their faith and it goes on attended by a great cloud of witnesses to challenge and inspire it. It has fostered education, nurtured scholars and furnished the churches with leaders of prophetic power and vision. It has by no means focused its worship entirely upon the spoken word, but for many reasons preaching has been its instrument and resource. Protestantism recognizes and claims the golden mouthed preachers of the Christian millenniums as part of its own inheritance, and it has added to that prophetic succession its own preachers of power and high distinction.

Its churches, great or small, throughout the English speaking world, are part of the near-to-life in all experiences and needs, in all that we share in common and cherish most. Without them the history of England, America, Germany and the Scandinavian peoples would have to be re-written and no one would know how to re-write it. Catholic is too spacious a word, too inclusive a conception to be restricted to any one Church order. Therefore, we believe that we are part of the fellowship of the Holy Catholic Church and our task is to continue, extend and exalt it. We may repeat, and many of our churches do, the oldest of the Christian creeds and confess with uncounted generations of Christian disciples "I believe in the Holy Catholic Church, the forgiveness of sins, the Communion of the Saints, the Resurrection of the Dead and the Life Everlasting. Amen."

* * *

There are many amongst us whose confidence in the future of American Protestantism is shaken, still others who consider it a losing cause, and all this for many reasons. To begin with its denominational differences trouble those who want efficiency and economy, or else are sensitive to the reproach of a divided church, or else would conceive of the church as the Mystical Body of Christ. The more practical see that Protestantism in so many regions demands a united front which it is not at present able to offer. They contrast it with the unity and discipline of the Roman Catholic Church with its dogmatic bases. The religious bases of Protestantism they think to have been weakened, perhaps by Biblical criticism, or likely by doctrinal doubts. Protestantism, therefore, offers less defense than a totalitarian system against the growing secularization of society. It is historically the bequest of an age of faith. It seems to lack the supports for an age of doubt. Its leaders watch uneasily those who turn to the assured shelter of an authoritarian church which supplies the answers, assumes responsibility for the lives of its communicants for time and eternity, and asks only their obediences and their loyalties, that they should receive its sacraments, be at peace through its absolution and kneel before its altars. There is no denying the very considerable force of all this.

Moreover, here in these United States, the historic primacy of Protestantism has been greatly altered, though this in a measure is regional. Protestantism is numerically a minority body in the whole of New England, and probably in most northern and eastern cities. Rural America has always been predominantly Protestant, and has supplied members and ministers to urban churches which have gradually lost the power of self-propagation. The out-populating power of the Protestant stock, long a statistically supported fact, seems to have been lost. Until the revision of our immigration laws Protestantism received a minor proportion of Protestant immigrants. All this I take to be an excess of despair. Actually, Protestantism is more than holding its own with the percentage growth of American population, a judgment on the basis of a more critical analysis of statistics since for the most part the Protestant Churches report only those actually on their lists of membership. America is still predominantly Protestant.

The Protestant Communions are uneven in their growth and gain. In general, denominations of evangelical fervor are outgrowing the churches which do not stress personal religious experience. The Churches whose worship is liturgical seem to hold and attract the young more markedly than the non-liturgical bodies. The strongly and centrally organized denominations seem to do better than the more loosely organized Communions. American Protestantism is on the whole theologically conservative. The Churches which have inherited and continue the spirit of free and critical inquiry do, at the best, little more than hold their own. The really arresting thing in American religious life is the growth and multiplication of small groups, variously and sometimes curiously named, who believe themselves in the true tradition of the Old and New Testaments. I think these churches are really the resource and comfort of the lonely, those lost in the vast anonymity of dismal city streets, of the partly socially disinherited, and of those haunted by fears. In all this they repeat the conditions in which Christianity itself began in the narrow streets of now vanished Greek and Roman cities.

* * *

It is strongly and increasingly held that without some form of organic church union, centrally organized, and authoritative, the future of American Protestantism is unhappily uncertain. Long steps in the direction of united action have al-

[17]

ready been taken and an overhead machinery begins to take form. Competent leaders offer a more closely knit federation as an alternative. That, they say, would be more simple, more immediately realizable, and far less likely to be attended by long drawn-out litigations over trust funds and property rights. Meanwhile, the tragic confusion of an endangered civilization overshadows everything. Christian missions were always, by every test, the best form in which our ways of life were offered to the Orient and the isles of the sea. The tragedies which have attended the entire Christian missionary enterprise cannot easily be put into words, as though there no longer are bridges of friendship and understanding left,—only bomb craters.

I recognize the gravity of the situation in which all Christian orders find themselves and the arrest of the Christian way in so many relationships of life where we carry on just as if Jesus had never lived and as if He had never died. To borrow from the manner of speech of the weather reports: the moral ceiling is low and visibility very limited. One must wait for clearing to see either high or far.

I do believe, however, that the very situations which seem to imperil Protestantism enhance its value for the present and the future. It was forged in travail and tempered in fire, an anvil which has worn out many hammers. All totalitarian orders have hitherto carried with them germs of their own undoing. They have broken through their rigidity. The very adaptability of Protestantism which has taken so many forms may prove to be one secret of its power to survive. Those who dared and who often greatly suffered to shape and maintain it, believed, in their various ways, that they were re-establishing Christianity upon its first foundation and in its apostolic spirit. Their experiences paralleled or repeated the experiences of Christianity in the days of its travail and spiritual splendor. It met and satisfied, and still meets and satisfies, the enduring needs of the questing human spirit. When freedom has become an embattled passion in the face of all that denies it, a mandate for freedom is the heritage of Protestantism and what seems to handicap it is the secret of its timeless power. The pendulum of history swings slowly and since the hour-hands of history circle a vast dial, the pendulum swings slow; but it is possible that we are due for a reaction along many fronts in a society where so many things are centered, patterned, ordered from above, and with little freedom of adaptation to individual circumstance. It may well be that in society, politics and religion the pendulum will swing back to the simple, the intimate and the self-initiated. If so, Protestantism will be ready and waiting. It holds in trust the liberties of Christian men and the hope of the Realm of God—not entirely, of course, but in ways of freedom and elasticity which may wonderfully suit a coming age.

* * *

Now that this article has used its allotted space I am sadly conscious of its faults of omission and maybe of commission. I have not written enough about the relations of Protestantism to the Bible. Its beginnings were co-eval with the movements which gave the people the Bible unchained and in their own tongue. Nor have I spoken enough of its leavening influence. It has created atmospheres and attitudes in which forms of religion alien to its own understanding have been changed and tempered. Its influence upon wide ranges of American thought cannot easily be put into words. Its leaders were men of profound religious conviction and they sought for all they did in doctrine and organization Biblical authority. Protestantism is still a Bible religion. The rights of private interpretation have been carried to fantastic limits, but for all that, the Bible has been the center in its now long and heroic history. I have touched a little—to repeat—on the ranges of its literature and the creation of free minds. Protestantism has always been particularly rich in devotional literature. And if there are two classics of Christian devotion, the *Imitation of Christ* and *Pilgrim's Progress,* John Bunyan has spoken for the seekers of long generations. And we may still stretch our hands across the sundering years and call Him brother.

The heritage of which I write is attested by a great cloud of witnesses. It, too, came up out of great tribulation and its saints and martyrs have won the right to sing the great doxologies.

* * *

I went to church this morning. In this instance it was a Community Church where men and women of many denominations work and worship together in a rare and beautiful fellowship. We sang together timeless hymns of faith and courage. We listened to one of the greatest psalms for a lesson. The prayers brought us into comradeship with one another and with God. The anthems were Scripture; the sermon was a call to courage and faith. Nothing could have been more essentially simple, more touched with the timeless, or more informed with the everlasting reality of religion; and yet there was hardly an element in the service which our right to use had not been purchased at a very great cost, a scarlet thread which ran through it all. The Christian order has left us many heritages, but this heritage of ours still stands strong against a shadowed sky and points to a light beyond the dawn. "A mighty fortress is our God, a bulwark never failing."

SUGGESTIONS FOR FURTHER READING

J. PAUL WILLIAMS, *What Americans Believe* (New York, 1952).

RAY FREEMAN JENNEY, *I am a Protestant* (Indianapolis, 1951).

HUGH THOMPSON KERR, *Positive Protestantism* (Philadelphia, 1950).

CHARLES CLAYTON MORRISON, *Can Protestantism Win America?* (New York, 1948).

J. MINTON BATTEN, *Protestant Backgrounds in History* (New York and Nashville, 1951).

Members of the Faculty of Union Theological Seminary in Virginia, *Our Protestant Heritage* (Presbyterian Committee of Publication of the Presbyterian Church, 1948).

MY PROTESTANT HERITAGE

ROLAND H. BAINTON, *The Reformation of the Sixteenth Century* (Boston, 1952).

————, *The Travail of Religious Liberty* (Philadelphia, 1951).
WILHELM PAUCK, *The Heritage of the Reformation* (Boston, 1950).
H. P. SMITH, *The Age of the Reformation* (New York, 1920).

(The writer of this chapter is in debt to the Rev. John A. Harrer, librarian of the Congregational Library of Boston, Mass., for important items in the bibliography; also to the admirable bibliography in Roland H. Bainton's *The Reformation of the Sixteenth Century.*)

THE JOY OF A GOOD CONSCIENCE

By

CONRAD HENRY MOEHLMAN

CONRAD HENRY MOEHLMAN

There is perhaps no living person more informed on the currently critical subject of the relation of church and state both from the religious and civil points of view than Dr. Moehlman. His great passion has been in recent years to educate Protestants on the importance of an understanding of this developed Protestant position and heritage and to stir them to action lest gains become losses. But this is not his major reputation. For decades he has taught at the Rochester Theological Seminary (now Colgate-Rochester Divinity School) in subjects relating to ancient languages undergirding the Christian tradition and especially in the history of the Christian church and its developing theologies and creeds. His books have been those typical of a scholar: carefully written, critical and original. He has helped Baptists to remember the genius of their heritage and to warn them of extravagances of accumulated interpretations. But not only to his own church has he ministered as only may a true scholar: he has pointed out the errors which were bound to accumulate in any biased ecclesiastical tradition and has fearlessly spoken out against them wherever they have become clear. His book titles show the range of his interests: "The Unknown Bible"; "What is Protestantism"; "The Catholic-Protestant Mind"; "The Story of Christianity"; "The American Constitutions and Religion"; "In Defense of the American Way of Life"; "Christianity and War"; "The Church as Educator"; "The Wall of Separation Between Church and State". There are many more. As a highly disciplined historian of the church from its infancy to its latest expressions, Professor Moehlman's estimate of Protestantism cannot fail to command our respectful reading and, if necessary, our own reorientation.

Editor

THE JOY OF A GOOD CONSCIENCE

Conrad Henry Moehlman

For me *it is necessary to postulate that religion cannot be destroyed.* It is so hoary with age; has accompanied man in all his frustrations to solve the riddle of his existence in his slow upward climb through the millennia; is so interwoven with all the cultural values from law and medicine and architecture and sculpture to alphabet, poetry, music, philosophy and ethics; originates on the border-line between the known and the unknown where mystery, wonder, awe, fear, and hope forever dwell; for hundreds of millions of persons still has the power of life and death; is unafraid of science because it has not and probably cannot solve the problem of what goes on after death; can always lift man out of his despair by promising a happier future; has almost infinite power to appropriate and synthesize contradictions by resorting to omnipotent allegorization, thus completely transforming its impossible traditions; urges weak man to move mountains by faith; atones for its weaklings and politicians and the mistakes of its theologians by growing prophets and saints; rises triumphantly from the dead after each final interment or cremation; is so sorely needed today that it seems destined to continue as long as man endures.

My second postulate is that despite the historian's inability to tell the story of religion, that he may only describe this and that in religion, that he may merely narrate only what religion has meant in the various cultures, he is nevertheless compelled to acknowledge on examining the cross-section of the religions of the world that some ideas are fairly common—such as the unity of the human race, the quest of God, the law written in the hearts of men, religion is faith expressing itself in love and the Golden Rule. Sooner or later in the growth of any religion, an ethical emphasis emerges and begins to compete with the more primitive religious values.

My third postulate is that humanity desperately demands a faith that love not hate is at the heart of the world, that love is superior to hate, that men must become brotherly in attitude and in practice or perish, that a law of service and of sacrifice underlies life, that a law of sowing and reaping is in the very structure of the universe, that happiness as an objective escapes our pursuit and comes only as an attendant ingredient of the good life, and that the only permanent reward from life is creative living.

Chester Firkins discovered that not even the roar of a subway express could efface his need of worship:

> I who have lost the stars, the sod,
>   For chilling pave and cheerless night,
> Have made my meeting place with God
>   A new and nether night—
> You that neath the country skies can pray,
>   Scoff not at me the city clod;
> My only respite of the day
>   Is this wild ride with God.

My fourth postulate is based on the discovery that the history of anthropology demonstrates that without pain there can be no progress for the race or the individual. Man cannot escape pain; cannot understand it; cannot suppress it; can only accept it not in self-pity but to put it to good use.

Even Nietzsche discerned this. He exalts those "who would rather have worse and greater hardships than ever before! Well-being as you conceive it—that is not an aim; for us it seems the end . . . The discipline of suffering, of *great* suffering—know you not that only *this* discipline has until now achieved all man's ascents? That tension of the soul in misfortune, which trains its strength; that shudder which seizes it in the presence of the great catastrophe; its resourcefulness and valiance in bearing, enduring, interpreting, utilizing misfortune; and whatever depth, mystery . . . shrewdness, greatness was ever granted to the soul—all this, was it not acquired through pain, in the school of great suffering?" (*Werke* VII, 180)

Hence, it has never been too difficult for me not to rebel against that revealing interpretation of Jesus by that gifted German scholar of pre-Hitler days, Wilhelm Bousset, that "for us his suffering, crucifixion and death are the crown and consummation of his life. We cannot conceive any ending to the life of Jesus grander, more powerful, or even other than it actually was. The cross and the crown of thorns do but complete his figure, and lift it far above those of the other founders of religions. Only by walking the appointed path of sorrow in silence and simplicity, without pretension and without faltering, in undiminished trust in his heavenly Father, in the unbroken conviction of his own divine mission, did he render his highest service. Only thus did he reveal the new moral world, ennoble suffering and defeat, and create the 'worship of sorrow' and the faith in the eternal value of martyrdom. Only here did he reach his consummation as leader of the ages and nations to God—for death and the grave could not hold his person and spirit."

My fifth postulate is that the age of organized religion is not ended despite Mr. Charles Wells' drawing and colloquy between the Little Brick Church and the Sky-scraper. "Said the Skyscraper to the Little Brick Church: 'You're looking smaller every day!' Replied the Little Brick Church: 'I've tried to keep close to the feet of men.' Continued the Skyscraper: 'But think of the progress you could have made if you had grown up like me and kept pace with the immense growth of this teeming city.' Said the Little Brick Church: 'I've tried to keep up with its broken hearts.' 'Yes,' spoke further the Skyscraper, 'but if you were up here you could see all over the city.' 'But here I can look into the worried faces that pass!' 'Yet you must realize,' voiced the Skyscraper, 'that I represent the wealth, power, and grandeur of modern civilization.' The

Little Brick Church thought a moment, then softly replied: 'But I have created the faith that held the wealth together, I've given purpose to the power and beauty of spirit to the grandeur.'

'My dear—you are weeping!' cried the Skyscraper.

'Forgive me. I didn't mean to'—chokingly replied the Little Brick Church—'but tomorrow they're tearing me down to make room for a movie palace.' "

My reasons for remaining within the Protestant fellowship in spite of its numerous insufficiencies and blindness to the signs of the times instead of joining the ranks of the unaffiliated stem from the conviction that "the joy of a good conscience" is the only goal worth pursuing to the end of the allotted span of years.

I

Religions are roughly classifiable as religions of authority and the religion of the spirit. Protestantism when and as it began was as authoritarian as the medieval religion from which it separated. Yet since it was the religious segment in the transition to the modern world, its abandonment of one element in the authoritarianism of the mother church denoted a weakening of the entire structure until the modern environment produced a series of new religious alignments. Protestantism has long since surrendered some of its earlier totalitarian claims. It has repented for what happened to Servetus. It admits that religion cannot be compelled and that it has not all of the truth in its confession of faith. It puts both the right and the responsibility for religious conclusions upon the individual. The "why judge ye not of yourselves what is right" is receiving more and more emphasis—at least in American Protestantism.

All this was brought home to me in a class-room experience toward the end of a half-century of teaching. The class in *Ethics* had assembled for the final period of the semester. It had considered historically, critically and psychologically the principal ethical problems confronting our troubled contemporary world and ourselves as well. In examining the numerous written student reflections from week to week, the instructor had become aware that the class had divided itself into two well-defined groups: one group was genuinely honest with the facts and itself, was personally grappling with the various issues; the other group was not anxious, troubled, concerned but at ease—with every problem solved, every issue settled, smug, confident, undoubtedly sleeping well at night after placing their questions in the proper pigeonholes.

The course was completed. I looked upon faces at ease and faces that were alert and wondering, as I summarized our findings. I could predict what those interested only in passing would *dogmatically* assert in their final papers. The "wasted" hours were over for them. Those who had visibly grown in ethical discernment would know throughout the years ahead what it means to accept individualism.

The bell rang. The last friendly farewells were spoken. But a considerable section of the class remained there huddled in a group. Evidently they too wished to express their gratitude to the instructor. They now approached *in a body and the appointed chairman spoke:* "Sir, we noticed all through the course how seriously you took all the arguments pro and con, never once compelling assent but attempting to make us reach our own conclusions, to judge for ourselves what was right. But we had no ethical problems to solve. We had long ago been given *the authoritative answers to these questions and needed not to concern ourselves with them. Had we done that, our whole religious structure would have come toppling down upon us.* But thanks and goodbye."

It was all so true! Authoritarian religion must make religion and ethics and economics and law and government into a program and code to be accepted without debate or it falls apart. It is the entire system that counts—take it or leave it. Time, however, takes its toll and the passing centuries make the program anachronistic and the exceptions to the ancient laws become so excessive that not even the theologians can decide the plain meaning of the code.

Consequently, the fear of disintegration drives an authoritarian religion to take protective measures, that is into an isolationism which at last becomes complete—separate schools, separate labor unions, separate reading materials, separate comics, separate cemeteries, and so on. But girls will be girls and insist upon falling in love with Alexander Mac Pherson instead of Dennis O'Reilly and the "other" schools, colleges, and universities appeal with such persuasive force that cultural effects cannot be overcome.

Precisely as no Constitution applied literally can meet the challenges of the unanticipated changes of the unknown future, as all Constitutions interpreted as programs fade away before the successive revolutionary modifications of custom and habit by environment, but interpreted as principles and ideals weather all change and survive as guiding stars from chaotic present situations to a securer future, so only the ethical understanding of religion which makes the individual a free man in his choice of direction can outlast change.

In other words, Protestantism does not have to take as much back because of the elements of personalism within it.

II

My first reason for being a member of a Protestant fellowship is personalism; my second reason is that it permits me not to draw a line between the sacred and the secular. In I Corinthians 12 is the classical statement for the unity of life. Even the doctors of medicine no longer reject the intimate connection between the *psyche* and the *soma*. The religion of Jesus did not recognize holy sections of time and space— seventh day versus the other six; Gerizim versus Jerusalem. Everything in life has value. I cannot agree with the Nietzsches, the Mussolinis, the Stalins, or misguided Americans who repeat and repeat that "the good are the nobles, the kings, the master races, the strong, the mighty, the rich and

that the evil are the meek, the poor, the weak." The proclamation of such wicked distinctions became in theory impossible when the universal priesthood of all believers was proclaimed. Certainly, in the Bible Belt "secular" ought not to be
heard so often since it isn't in the Bible.

In Genesis 1:27 it is written: So God formed man in his
own likeness . . . and blessed them; in Genesis 1:31; And
God saw *all* that he had made *and it was very good;* the
standard of the Rule of God is the Golden Rule; the sun
shines and the rains fall upon the evil and the good. Nothing
is "secular" according to Acts 10:10-16. The "secular" social
workers are placed at the right hand to receive their deserved
reward in Matthew 25 while the pious are surprised to find
themselves on the left side. Those who respect the Lord's
Prayer ought to remember that the word translated "daily"
has been found only in the "secular" vocabulary of the time.
Christian scholars were accustomed to claim it as a specifically
religious coinage of the early church and often insisted it was
found only at Luke 11:3, Matthew 6:11, and in the Didache
8:2. Alas, alas! it is now demonstrated to have been a "sordid
commercial business word", a memorandum of expenses for
"ordinary things" like straw and peas. Think of it, the *religious* vocabulary of the Lord's Prayer does not hesitate to use
a completely "secular" term. This ought to reduce the theologian's fondness for decrying the "secularism" they find in
contemporary life.

In his *Christianity and Democracy,* Jacques Maritain alleges
that the tragedy of democracy has been its repudiation of the
Gospel and Christianity in the name of liberty, but then is
compelled to acknowledge that the modern apostles of social
emancipation could not discover Jesus within the church because they could do no other than equate religious orthodoxy
with political and religious oppression and adds that Fascism
"dechristianized the Church herself." Democracy, Maritain
continues, is a "temporal manifestation of the gospel". But
did not the church oppose the labor movement of 1848 in

France? It was, he admits, the "hidden work of evangelical inspiration" which deposited seven values upon the "secular conscience", namely, faith in progress, faith in the rights of the individual, the sense of human equality, that earthly rulers derive their authority from the people, the condemnation of power politics, the sense of the inalienable freedom of man, the sense of human brotherhood.

Likewise, Reinhold Niebuhr pauses to remark that "it must be recognized that the impulse toward the achievement of justice and brotherhood in the past two centuries has frequently been borne primarily by the secularists who emphasized the petition which Christians had neglected: *Thy Kingdom* Come . . ."

Berggrav, war-time bishop of Oslo noticed that Matthew 5:10 and Matthew 5:11 identify "to suffer for the sake of righteousness" with "to suffer for Jesus' sake", commenting that "there are no such things as 'secular' matters for a Christian conscience."

It was when Martin Luther made the common task a "vocation", a "calling" and refused to recognize a thesaurus of merit that the walls of medieval piety came tumbling down.

The aberration of Protestantism in rejecting so much of the good life of today and in alienating so many of the extra-denominational champions and defenders of the infinite significance of human life can only be temporary. Only God was good for Jesus, but that did not prevent him from associating with even the "collectors of internal revenue" of Pilate's administration. Karl Barth's devaluation of man to "wholly other" and to absolute insignificance helped the German people to accept Hitler. When Protestantism fully returns to the gospel of Jesus, it will restore man to that level of dignity, glory, sense of service and of brotherhood and of responsibility which will create in him a new desire to become a maintainer of peace instead of a manufacturer of the weapons of war and an instrument of hate.

III

My third reason for being a Protestant is that it enables me personally to feel a sense of guilt for the failures of these recent decades.

The *omnes peccavimus* of Paul has been woefully misinterpreted. As I read Romans I find that he assigns my guilt to me against the background of the failures of my day and age. My guilt consists in not fighting all the day against the evils I found in the world since 1879. Mr. Justice William O. Douglas expresses my own convictions so well that I quote: "These days I see graft and corruption reach high into government. These days I see people afraid to speak their minds because someone will think they are unorthodox and therefore disloyal. These days I see America identified more and more with material things, less and less with spiritual standards. These days I see America drifting from the Christian faith, acting abroad as an arrogant, selfish, greedy nation . . . interested only in guns and dollars . . . not in people and their hopes and aspirations. These days . . . we need the faith that dedicates us to something bigger and more important than ourselves or our possessions. Only if we have that faith will we be able to guide the destiny of the nations, in this the most critical period of world history."

The cure of my guilt cannot be found in the fifth century dogma of original sin. This Augustinian proposal is neither biblical nor honest, lacking all historical support as far as Judaism and early Christianity are concerned. It has so confused and retarded the growth of the corporate ethical conscience of Christianity that all Protestant groups must come to grips with it. The horrible assumption that my children could be guilty of an assumed ancient sin, that "Adam's guilt" could be physically transmitted from generation to generation by parents, whose parents, whose parents . . . whose parents for all the generations had been freed from it by baptism not only staggers the imagination but has so damaged the concept of marriage, fatherhood, and motherhood that only the authority of the church enables it to be ritualistically continued.

A study of the ethical quadrilateral of Jesus with its demand of justice, and love and humility and heroism, where humility is the oughtness of strength and heroism what justice and love require in the presence of injustice produce such a consciousness of guilt within me that Augustine's "discovery" becomes meaningless and it is impossible to accept Anna-case-ethics, where Anna was an adulteress and is shown so convincingly by a theologian how she may lie three times to prevent her husband from discovering the fact by use of "semantics".

Only as I have judged myself severely have I been able occasionally to prevent myself from "willingly planting a thorn in another man's bosom".

In Protestantism, I have had the freedom to experiment with the processes of building character, discovering that those who helped me associated themselves with my pain and agony and doubt. Indeed, no one can participate in the redemption of the world who has not felt its shortcomings and mistakes within himself.

In the late 1920s my personal conclusions were confirmed by the testimony of Albert Schweitzer in that passage where he tells why he had to go to Africa to become a medical missionary to the people in Lambarene, equatorial Africa: "A heavy guilt rests upon our culture! What have not the whites of all nations since the era of discovery done to the colored peoples! What does it signify that so many peoples whither Christianity came have died out and others are vanishing or are at least distintegrating? Who will describe the injustices and atrocities committed by Europeans? Who would estimate what alcohol and the awful diseases we transmitted to them have done to them? If history were to tell all that has happened between whites and blacks, many pages would be turned without reading them. A heavy guilt rests upon us . . .

We must serve them. When we do good to them, it is not benevolence, it is expiation, it is repentance."

IV

My fourth reason for feeling at home in Protestantism is that by emphasizing this personal ethical quality in Christianity, it produces a solid basis for a social gospel.

I was never at ease when reflecting upon the five points of Calvinism. "Jesus lover of my soul" always meant much more to me than "Rock of Ages" and how deep-seated the original difference between the two hymns was is soon discovered by the church historian. But budding theologians cannot recognize those antitheses today and my father's hyper-Calvinistic church sang them in succession with the same vigor. This could only be because the Arminian heresy in the former had been rubbed out in the experience of these pious and orthodox German Baptists. They had overcome the original antitheses because their ethical reaction had made an unconscious unity of the two hymns for them as individuals.

I was taught at my mother's knee how true *Pilgrim's Progress* was. But my aversion to the five points of Calvinism made it impossible to enjoy Bunyan's masterpiece and the tinker's immortal allegory made no deep religious impression upon me. Then came a very belated awakening, namely, that for the common man of Bunyan's day that allegory was "a program for action and not for meditation, that hundreds of workers, farmers, and merchants found nightly reinvigoration by reading Bunyan, and went out in the morning refreshed with the assurance that by making a shoe, or plowing a furrow, or raising the interest rate they were conquering "Apollyon" and thus they attained peace of mind.

Max Weber gave the departure of Adam and Eve from Paradise a new significance when he interpreted Milton as affirming that it meant a new life, a conquest by the spirit of man over his less significant earlier life.

[35]

"Men may cry out against sin in the pulpit but carry it around with them in the heart."

And I recall how a consistent Calvinist teacher of mine made the system over by asserting that there was no conflict between Paul and James, that Calvinism taught that good works were fruitage, were the necessary result of the new life produced within the Christian by his experience of salvation but never acts done to merit salvation. A Christian was one who *desired* to do good because of his experienced love of God. No scale-pan view of God, said he, could be found in the New Testament.

Similarly, Thoreau reinterpreted the Gospel of Jesus into socio-ethical terms for me, when I read this: "The New Testament is an invaluable book, though I confess to having been slightly prejudiced against it in my early days by the church and the Sabbath school, so that it seemed, before I read it, to be the yellowist book in the catalogue . . .

"It is remarkable, that notwithstanding the unusual favor with which the New Testament is outwardly received, and even the bigotry with which it is defended, there is no hospitality shown to, there is no appreciation of the order of truth with which it deals. I know of no book that has so few readers. There is none so truly strange and heretical and unpopular. To Christians, no less than to Greeks and Jews, it is foolishness and a stumbling-block. There are, indeed, severe things in it no man should read aloud but once. 'Seek ye first the kingdom of heaven,' 'Lay not up for yourselves treasure on earth,' 'If thou wilt be perfect, go and sell that thou hast, and give to the poor.' 'For what is a man profiteth, if he shall gain the whole world and lose his own soul? or what shall a man give in exchange for his soul?' Think of this, Yankees! 'Verily I say unto you, if ye have faith as a grain of mustard seed, ye shall say unto this mountain, Remove hence to yonder place; and it shall remove; and nothing shall be impossible unto you.' Think of repeating these things to a New England audience! Thirdly, fourthly, fifteenthly, till there are three

barrels of sermons! Who, without cant, can read them aloud?
Who, without cant, can hear them, and not go out of the
meeting house? They never *were* read, they never *were* heard.
Let but one of these sentences be rightly read from any pulpit
in the land and there would not be left one stone of that
meeting-house upon another."

The ethicizing of the plan of salvation, however faultily
carried out in practice, grants to each individual a better opportunity to fuse his personal ethics with a social ethic into a
satisfactory social attitude and activity than the vain attempt
to turn Jesus into a twentieth century sociologist and philosopher which he never pretended to be and early Christians into
supporters of an ideology which they could not have grasped
even if it could have been presented to them.

V

My fifth reason for endorsing Protestantism is associated
with the fact that it has confessions of faith but not authoritarian dogmas in the earlier sense. The point is decisive. It is the
difference between *credo* and *credendum,* between personal
faith and what must be accepted of an ecclesiastical, authoritarian deliverance. "Not Credo but Amo." "The overwhelming need in every age has been the deed of good will instead
of the creed of exclusion." The penalties imposed in authoritarian religions to secure conformance have disintegrated into
appeal, persuasion, and recognition of variety and pluralism
as salutary in Protestantism.

For example, Thomas à Kempis sought the solution of his
problem in withdrawal, attempting to escape from the kingdom of God among men by the kingdom of God within himself—"the purification of his individual soul" in solitude and
solitariness. Thackeray rightly concluded that "the scheme [of
the *Imitation*] carried out would make the world the most
wretched, useless, dreary, doting place of sojourn . . . a set of
selfish beings, crawling about, avoiding one another and howl-
ing a perpetual *Miserere*."

Nevertheless, rejecting his description of life as something to be accepted as dogma, one can appreciate what à Kempis was seeking, for it is precisely what we also seek in different ways—"the joy of a good conscience". He *remade* the creed of his church in the experience of his life.

The *Westminster Confession of Faith* was taken over almost verbatim by Congregationalists and by Baptists and abides to this day in these democratic fellowships but note well what took place. The creeds and dogmas of medieval Christianity became mere Confessions of Faith, which in turn became Declarations and local covenants and signing your name in a church register until for the laity in Protestantism creeds are often unread and antiquated documents which are only inherited symbols but cannot be required or enforced in any significant way. The *gerundive* of the medieval creeds has surrendered unconditionally to the *indicative* of the individual's faith. Creeds as dogmas are in many Protestant bodies gathering dust in the archives. If some Confessions of Faith were read in some worship services without comment, the laity would be startled to discover what their spiritual ancestors had believed.

VI

My sixth reason for supporting the Protestant way is that Protestantism feels at home in a democratic environment and an age of science. Indeed, it had much to do with laying the religious foundation for both democracy and science. Since the sixteenth century more progress in democracy and science has occurred than in the centuries between Augustine and Luther.

Because Protestantism had appealed to the Bible it had to face the facts its scholars were uncovering. The Latin Bible gradually was replaced by a more critical Hebrew text in the Old Testament and a Greek text in the New Testament. As earlier manuscripts became known and their disagreements multiplied, text anarchy had to be solved by development of critical study and choice had to be made from variant meanings. But new texts led to new interpretations. Archaeology insisted upon being heard. The sands of Egypt yielded barrels of papyri occasionally with sayings of Jesus until the results of all these studies escaped from the esoteric environment of the theological institutions into the sermons preached in some pulpits and thus the Bible's strata and growth of the collection of the separate books could no longer be ignored.

A critical text demanded new versions and the Revised Version, the American Revised Version, countless translations by one scholar or many adding this and that new insight gave birth to a Bible so different from the medieval Christian Bible that conservative divinity schools in the interest of more fully understanding the Bible became the chief propagandists of the countless variations in the different Bibles and the separate manuscripts. Hence, the Bible of today is not the Bible of yesterday. The questions regarding the structure of the four gospels and of the Pentateuch, regarding the authorship of the first five books of the Old Testament, of the Hebrew Bible being divided into Law, Prophets, Writings, of the origin of Daniel in the second century B.C., of the Gospel of Mark beginning his narrative of the life of Jesus with John the Baptizer, of Mark 16:9-20 missing in the older manuscripts, of John 7:53-8:11 also missing, of I John 5:7 of the King James Bible not found in any Greek manuscript which has not been retouched—a thousand questions like these must finally be answered by every scholar. And the contradictory answers compel even authoritarian churches to issue revisions of the Bible. Stalwart Karl Barth was unable to answer the searching questions put to him by Adolf Harnack and became an enigma to his disciples by the constructions he put upon the Bible to obtain his subjective results.

The contemporary culture-pattern which Christianity has helped weave cannot be conquered by shouting "secularism" or by isolationism. To maintain connection with the contemporary spiritual life and certainly to exert any influence upon it, Christianity must solve modern man's enigmas.

For Protestantism, some new thinking is possible, some new helpful contributions may be made, if it will but endorse:

> *Let me die thinking.* Let me fare forth still with
>   an open mind,
> Fresh secrets to unfold, new secrets to find,
> My soul undimmed, alert, no question blinking:
> *Let me die thinking.*

VII

My seventh reason for assuming that Protestantism's mission is by no means ended stems from the endless varieties it has and is still producing. Without multiplicity of sects and cults, religious freedom would vanish and liberty of conscience would be reduced to an external conformance. If one must choose between the oddities, the ravings, the screamingly contradictory mouthings of religious enthusiasm and authoritarian decrees of self-appointed religious bureaucracies and dictatorships, much could be said in favor of the voluntary way. Fringe groups point up the mistakes of some Protestant preaching, the ineffectiveness of attempting to frighten the modern man by shouting "hell-fire" for which the cultist can substitute "holy-fire" and group happiness. I tuned in this morning to hear a leader of a "holiness group" shout: "I was happy, very happy in my life of sin. Thank God, I find I can be just as happy in the Jesus way." It reminded me of receiving, because of confusion of schools some three decades ago, a letter from a spinster in a Southern state who desired to join a Northern religious group and enclosed a number of her poems describing how wicked she was. Think it over.

Education can reduce our endless religious varieties but first many changes must be effected in our major religious groups. After a few decades of counselling, many will discover how the personal approach has brought harmony where there was chaos and religious democracy when there was anarchy and rebellion.

There can be religious unity within religious diversity, if

only there is sympathetic and intelligent understanding of the causes of the multiplicity of sects. Ecumenicity by coercion means a greater number of sects and cults. The questions always come back to the separate religious fellowships for approval, and some of our American leaders in ecumenicity are expressing misgivings about the eschatological emphasis in European Protestantism. Opinions men bring into a conference usually are brought back home again. But the despised sects of yesteryears became the powerful denominations of the next century.

Possibly it is worth remembering that Celsus found many varieties of Christians in his day but the Roman Empire was unable to suppress their common faith.

The guarantee of freedom of conscience and of religion is not in compelled conformance but in voluntary choice and approval. At any rate, "where the Spirit of the Lord is, there is liberty."

VIII

My eighth reason for attempting to advance Protestantism is what has been described as "the greatest contribution made to the science of government by the western world", namely, the religious clause of the First Amendment to the Constitution of the United States. Without the initiative of American Protestantism the theory of the separation of church and state could not have originated.

Protestantism was the religious phase of the transition to the modern world. It was intimately tied in with geographical discovery, commerce, the rebellion against the medieval ecclesiastical control of the economic life which issued in what is today called the free enterprise system, the system of economic liberalism of that day, with the assertion of the rights of the individual against ecclesiastical collectivism, with freedom of conscience. As the Virginia Declaration of Rights put it: "All men are equally entitled to the free exercise of religion according to the dictates of conscience" or as it is written in the

Virginia Bill for Establishing Religious Freedom, a decade later: "No man shall be compelled to frequent or support any religious worship, place or ministry whatsoever, nor shall be enforced, restrained, molested or burthened in his body or goods nor shall otherwise suffer on account of his religious opinions or belief; but all men shall be free to profess and by argument to maintain their opinions in matters of religion, and that the same shall in no wise, diminish, enlarge or affect their civil capacities."

When these concepts were written into the Northwest Ordinance, the Constitution and its First Amendment, with the help of Protestantism and were anchored in the American mores during the following one and one-half centuries, Protestantism took a tremendous risk but in the end performed an incomparable task in the history of western religion.

And the people of the western world ratified this accomplishment by growing a more vital religion in America than Europe has ever known and by demonstrating that union of church and state in the modern world must in the end prove a miserable failure.

For supporting the slogan that "all men have a natural and unalienable right to worship Almighty God according to the dictates of their own conscience," and refusing to be enticed to compromise with ecclesiastical power to gain political power, Protestantism has always had my vote.

IX

And this unique separation of church and state American principle has as its necessary corollary, universal public education which is my ninth reason for humbly calling myself a Protestant. Public education in its contemporary significance is the child of the American Constitution. It is of the genius of American democracy, for only general intelligence can suffice to maintain the morality, political strength and efficiency and understanding vital for a democracy. When surveys showed that 80 percent of the criminals were produced in

New England in the 1870s by the 7 percent of illiterate population and in New York City there was one crime for every three among illiterates but only one crime for every twenty-seven among those who had received public school training, that in 1879 in Pennsylvania, the less than four percent of illiterate population accounted for one-third of all the crime, Americans began to appreciate why the Founding Fathers placed such an emphasis upon the "general intelligence".

The public schools are for all American children; do not discriminate between the right and wrong side of the track; are controlled by the people and therefore supported by public taxes which I just as gladly pay today as when our own youngsters attended them; are without religious tests for teachers or pupils; are without denominational bias or sectarian instruction or "structured religion" emphasis; opposed to becoming defenders of this or that sectarian tenet but wholeheartedly committed to the inculcation of ethical religious principles.

President Grant was so right when he said: "Encourage free schools and resolve that not one dollar appropriated for their support shall be appropriated to the support of any sectarian schools. Resolve that either the state or the nation, or both combined, shall support institutions of learning sufficient to afford to every child growing up in the land the opportunity of a good common school education, unmixed with sectarian, pagan, or atheistical dogmas. Leave the matter of formal religion to the family circle, the church, and the private school supported entirely by private contributions. Keep the church and state forever separate."

Formal religious training apparently does not always succeed in producing character. Let us quote from a few students of juvenile delinquency: "It is a curious fact, however, that the states and sections of our own country where religious 'fundamentalism' shows the fewest signs of collapse are the states and sections which have the heaviest ratios of the most serious crimes and which have proportionately produced the greatest

[43]

number of criminals." Eighty percent of prison inmates (the sample was 85,000) expressed a preference for Christianity.

If formal religion can be taught, why do surveys made to determine the effectiveness of the Sunday School show a ratio of .002 between a child's development and what he has learned in Sunday School? Professor G. H. Betts summarizes the Hartshorne-May investigation thus: "From extensive tests given many children in such traits as cheating and copying in school work, telling lies about their own achievements, taking unfair advantage of others, etc., no relation was found between such conduct and the numbers in Sunday School attendance. Non-attendants made as good a record as regular attendants.

"Character traits investigated by the same men among other groups of children were: kindness and helpfulness, loyalty to their group, generosity, self-control. Here again no relation to Sunday School attendance was found, or so slight a relation as to be negligible.

"The correlation of moral knowledge [knowledge of right and wrong] with Sunday School attendance was slightly negative. In one high-grade neighborhood it was found that those who never attended Sunday School made a better score on the character tests than those who attended somewhat regularly."

I am proud that Protestantism assisted at the birth and the development of Public Education.

X

Finally, I am a Protestant because it possesses the qualities of youth; daring to face the future; being optimistic in spite of occasional lapses into pessimism and attempts to escape existing problems. It cannot finally agree with the Malayan convert to Christianity whom Maxwell Anderson describes as crying to the Malayan gods before drinking the cup of poison: "He came too soon, this Christ of peace. Men are not ready yet. Another hundred thousand years they must drink your potion of tears and blood."

Rather it believes that Gibran was nearer right when he wrote:

> Work is love made visible.
> And if you cannot work with love but only with distaste, it is better that you should leave your work and sit at the gate of the temple and take alms of those who work with joy.
> For if you bake bread with indifference, you bake a bitter bread that feeds but half a man's hunger.

And this from Benjamin Kidd's *Science of Power* deserves consideration: "The idealism of mind and spirit conveyed to the young of each generation under the influence of *the social passion* is absolutely limitless in its effects. The power which is represented thereby is capable of creating a new world in the lifetime of a generation. It is capable of sweeping away in a single generation any existing order in the world—evidence Germany under Hitler, and Russia under Lenin and Stalin."

I often in hours of discouragement reread this from Ross commenting upon the quotation from Gibran: "Gibran might have been writing this directly to ministers or theological students. How many work with enthusiasm, joy, love? How many have succumbed to the postures of professionalism?

"Modern man seems to have lost the meaning of *vocation* —being called to a task that fulfills the total man even as it meets a genuine social need. The minister is frequently caught in this same realm of meaninglessness, where he tries to find the meaning of his calling in the results or expected rewards of his labors.

"To *labor* is to pray. *To do the work that one is built to do, to do it with joy, this is life's richest fulfillment*. Life is a pilgrimage: results are not predictable. To work and to work alone is man entitled, never to its rewards . . . *Wretched is he who works for results. To find himself through creative work—it is to this that each man is called.*

"Let me die working, still tackling plans unfinished tasks undone! Clean to its end, swift may the race be run. No laggard steps, no faltering no shirking! *Let me die working!*"

I imagine the young men who helped Goethals dig the Panama Canal complained many a time against food, flies, heat, housing, bugs, and more bugs. But their deeds inspired someone to let them sing: "Don't send us back to a life that's tame again. We, who have shattered a continent's spine. Office work? Oh! we couldn't do that again. Haven't you something that's more in our line? Got any rivers they say are not crossable? Got any mountains you can't tunnel through? We specialize in the wholly impossible. Doing what nobody ever could do."

Let Protestantism keep faith with ongoing life directing it into paths of justice, love, humility, and the heroism which makes for peace and not dreading to leave its "outgrown shell by Time's unresting sea" and it can build the "more stately mansions" and the "nobler temples" of life.

What, then, is the upshot of our discussion? A Protestantism which makes Jesus a theological cross-word puzzle or the materialized God of the raised wafer of the communion sacrament cannot redeem the oncoming generations of men. But a Protestantism that dares to grapple with the new problems of the present age on the basis of ethical considerations found in the Bible from Genesis to Revelation can win.

David S. Muzzey accurately describes our time in these words:

> If our country needed a new birth of freedom in Lincoln's day, how much greater is that need today! We are struggling in the shackles of bondage which bewilderment, fear, materialism, suspicion and spiritual apathy have fastened upon us. We long for the peace in which alone liberty can flourish; yet, we are faced everywhere with strife and mutual distrust and recrimination. Perjured testimony before courts and investigating committees knows no limit but the wit-

ness's calculation of how much he can "get away with". The general welfare of the people is of negligible importance in the struggles of labor and capital for a larger share of the country's wealth. The chronic crisis of war and rumors of war has produced a creeping paralysis of fear in our political leaders, who vainly trust that somehow peace will be the final goal of stockpiling ever more murderous bombs. And millions of us common citizens, longing for deliverance from the shackles of bondage, are distressed by the seeming impotence of our efforts to counter policies which threaten the fanning of the "cold war" into the flames of a gigantic holocaust. Where shall we find relief from our forebodings and release from the anxieties that cloud our vision of a world set free from the base rivalries of recrimination and reprisal, of prejudice and persecution, of mutual suspicion and slaughter? How shall we save our own souls alive in the midst of the public and private betrayals of the moral law which disgrace our society?

An ethically oriented Protestantism is sufficient for this Herculean labor.

SUGGESTIONS FOR FURTHER READING

W. E. GARRISON, *A Protestant Manifesto* (Nashville, 1951).

ADOLF VON HARNACK, *What is Christianity?* (New York, 1901).

PERRY MILLER, *Jonathan Edwards* (New York, 1949).

AUGUSTE SABATIER, *Religions of Authority and the Religion of the Spirit* (New York, 1904).

ERNST TROELTSCH, *Protestantism and Progress* (New York, 1912).

AFFIRMATIVE PROTESTANTISM

By

FRANCIS JOHN MCCONNELL

Francis John McConnell

Beloved bishop of the Methodist Church (elected in 1912), and long a senior bishop, Dr. McConnell is a notable name in American Protestantism. A doctor of philosophy from Boston University, he holds many honorary degrees (Ohio Wesleyan, Wesleyan University, Yale, Boston) and has taught at many institutions of learning (Columbia, Drew, Garrett, Yale) besides holding many responsible posts in ecclesiastical circles, notably president of the Federal Council of Churches of Christ (1929). His appointment to significant lectureships attest to the regard he has been held by academic faculties here and abroad. Few persons in the Christian church have had the rare combination which he has possessed and which mark his distinguished ministry: he has been a prophet in spite of the priestly functions conferred upon him. Always socially spirited, he has stood out fearlessly for a gospel with social implications. Philosophically minded, he has had the characteristic forward look as becomes a philosopher, taking a stand for progressive movements of thought in spite of the conservatism of ecclesiasticism. An admirer of Borden P. Bowne he has helped to popularize the typically American philosophy of personalism. His books have been exceedingly popular through the years—because, it is sure, he is never obscure and dull and, what is more, because he has always been provocative. Among his many books are "The Divine Immanence" (1906); "Democratic Christianity" (1919); "Is God Limited?" (1924); "The Christlike God" (1927); "The Christian Ideal and Social Control" (1933); "Evangelicals, Revolutionists and Idealists" (1942). Bishop McConnell's interpretation of Protestantism, from the perspective of many solid years in its service, cannot help being a pronouncement of inestimable value.

Editor

AFFIRMATIVE PROTESTANTISM

Francis John McConnell

THOSE of us who have lived long in any Protestant religious community have been at times impressed, if not depressed, when we hear Protestant churches spoken of as preaching a "No Gospel", that is to say a negative gospel telling us that as members of a church there are so many things we must not do. As one who has passed the age of fourscore, it gives me great pleasure to say that I have seen the emphasis in the Protestant message pass so largely to sermons which tell us not so much of what we ought not to do but so much of what we can do and ought to do.

There are many reasons why Protestantism of the older type put its stress on what we ought not to do. The Protestant beliefs, as Protestant beliefs, were born largely in a battle atmosphere. They were formed and developed in the presence of what the leaders thought of as an enemy, that is to say for purposes of attack, attack which called forth energies and heroic resistance. It was easy, or seemed easy, to the Protestant fighters to point to wrong, or doubtful, beliefs or deeds, which naturally led to preaching against courses which the Protestants thought must be strenuously denounced. It was not hard, for instance, to denounce the sale of indulgences, for such sales oftentimes produced evil consequences which were not matters of insight but of eyesight.

Or to take a more important illustration. We may think of the emphasis the earlier churches placed on cathedral-building. It is now hard to see just what there was in a cathedral to warrant attack by Protestant Christians, but the pulpit orators found plenty. They thought of the emphasis on these majestic buildings as savoring too much of materialism, to say nothing of religious magic. The physical protection given a fugitive from secular justice at the door of a cathedral was compounding with state iniquity. The use of any but the simplest musical instruments in religious worship was condemned as wicked till within the memories of our own times. We all, or most of us, now think of a cathedral built long before the Reformation as one of the noblest expressions of Christianity in fact and symbol. The cathedral was built to last. There was nothing commonplace about it. On an appropriate site it could be seen for miles. No matter what the dull spectator thought about it, one glance at it told what it was for and something of its finer meaning. Its creation came out of the cooperative effort of a community and every dweller in sight of it was proud of it; and every traveler in lands far distant from it who had passed his boyhood near it felt a warming of his heart, as his memory stirred at the thought of its towers and walls and buttresses and bells, and its ritual processions. It makes little difference that in the early days of the Reformation period the Protestants missed much of this. They for a time cared only for what they called the inwardly spiritual. This was all sincere enough. It may be that those defenders of Protestantism were correct in thinking of a force of religious imagination so vivid that it could people the little chapels with hosts of heavenly multitudes, but, even so, something was missing.

Now what the ardent Protestant was likely to forget was that the spiritual qualities which sum up the religious legacies of old times were indeed his legacies as well as the inheritance of those whom he so often thought of as his enemies, and the Lord's enemies. The weightier doctrines which we proudly think of as essentially and peculiarly our own had taken their form, though not their expression, long before Protestantism had begun to stir. Probably it would be just to say that every one of the creeds which the early Christian Fathers shaped has in it phrases that the church has not been able to improve upon since they were first written.

Now it is necessary to say, after this possibly overwrought recognition of the religious legacy which the earlier church sent down to all after ages, that Protestantism finally got over the fighting spirit far enough to begin to see the vastness of the Christian inheritance which was Christian from the beginning, and has perhaps given its more important efforts in attempting to carry out the Christian system into its implications and applications. There are different methods of studying a prophet or his prophecy. One method is to ask what the prophet says and let it go at that. The other method is to ask what the prophecy means beyond its direct utterance. One way to understand Jesus is to ask what Jesus taught, and to seek all the light we can on what he did say. Another way is to ask the meaning of what he said for our own day and the days to come after.

If I may hazard a word here on a controversial theme, may I say it seems to me there is one difference between Roman Catholic and Protestant religious teaching. I do not intend here to enter the field of political discussion, but I cannot help thinking that Roman Catholic utterance seems to belong to the realm of command, to be obeyed, rather than a revelation to be studied. In one case we deal with a general and in the other with a teacher.

I once had the privilege of talking with a Roman Catholic bishop over the problem of papal decrees. He explained to me their freedom from error. I replied to him that I could not see the difference between a papal decree and a decree like that of our Supreme Court, except in the number of the judges. Practically, that makes a good deal of difference, for the Catholic claim is that the decision is the sure result of one mind, whereas the decision by a court of a dozen or more does not seem to be so sure. This, however, is a matter of opinion. The Pope can claim that he speaks with the voice of God, which he claims that no other human voice can pass upon. My Catholic friend finally closed our discussion by challenging me to point out one papal decree which has been mistaken. Personally, I thought that the doctrine of decrees itself had been mistaken. I do not wish to be flippant about such an affair, but I wonder how anybody could ever show that the most recent papal decree, that concerning the Assumption of the Virgin Mary, could be proved. The safety for the above decree is partly that we never can find the historic truth in such a case, and further, that it makes no great difference whether we can ever find such a proof. The Roman Catholic faithful will believe the decree chiefly for purposes of worship and for expected answer to prayer, but that is not proof in the sense in which we are now talking.

The most essential question in this field is as to what practical, matter-of-fact difference in actual relation to religious results, the answer, one way or the other, could make.

We are trying to think of Protestantism from the angle of affirmations, without now passing judgment on the final quality of the applications. Even when Protestant groups make policies which later history shows to have been mistaken, we have often to admit that the mistakes have been remediable. Protestantism has a deal to say about its determining and controlling and constructive force in economic realms in lands where it has had adequate power. To look at a somewhat unusual claim, think of the force today claimed for even extreme Calvinism in the development of the capitalistic system. John Calvin is not before my mind as an especially amiable character; he was a dictator of the most extreme type. We will not stop to try to show that there was in his day a host of dictators more dictatorial than he. He, however, made an outstanding blunder in his attitude on the burning of Servetus. There is today some question as to how far Calvin was responsible for that judicial murder. We may well believe, however, that he could have stopped the execution if he had so desired. Some students have supposed that Calvin could have saved Servetus if he had known that Servetus was a scientist, busy with experiments as to the circulation of the blood. This may be a bit far-fetched, for very possibly Calvin would have believed any theory of the circulation of the blood to be of no worth compared with his own theology as to the inner relationships of the Divine Trinity.

Let that pass however. I call attention to the fact that Calvin was a devoted and a terribly fierce defender of the doctrine of human predestination. I use this illustration in face of the fact that the doctrine is not today in favor like that it once enjoyed. It had, however, a vast strength in the days when the civilization of the time was seething everywhere with new problems in just about every field of human thought and enterprise. In those enormously vital days Calvin's doctrine of a divine calling for men in every and any field which they thought worthy of the divine attention, gave them a consciousness of strength, through consciousness of the cooperation with the Divine Will, which strengthened all of them, and made some of them all but irresistible. Take the history of New England, for example. Very few of us today would have cared to live on the same street or in the same town with these Calvinists. To speak paradoxically, even their positive was likely to have the force of a negative through human resentment at their tyranny.

I do not need to speak of the excess of these leaders as builders of states, here in America, let us say. I am thinking more especially of the effect of their calling men to a life work, or an earthly "business career" that was characteristic of the time. If a man seeking for control over his fellowmen in material business or in any work-a-day relation came to believe that God was back of and approving everything he did, he felt free to do much that one without a theology made for earthly success would never have thought of attempting. Any worldly success that the industrial leader might meet could confirm his conviction as to the truth of divine calling in his life. If he was ever inclined to raise a question as to the soundness of his predestination theology, he was likely, in the midst of strenuous search for control of material forces, not to worry himself about theology, especially of the metaphysical form.

Of course, all these monsters of successful enterprises created a problem for the after times. It is difficult to tell how much the Protestantism of Protestant leaders counted for productive results until public opinion had become organized into political parties. Luther had rather close connections with the people who followed him at all, but it is not easy to tell how large these followings were. Outside what might have been a growing popular interest in national affairs, Luther seems not himself to have been interested in human welfare as such, though this judgment is based on his support of the ruling classes in the Peasants' Revolt, which is indeed a dark passage in Luther's record.

When we come to the period of the great American settlements, especially, we find rising tides of interest in church movements in which various forces of Protestantism played the decisive part, largely because so many of these groups had back of them English antecedents. The work of Wycliffe was familiar to English settlers, and Wycliffe's career was part of the inheritance which the English carried, at least in their minds, in their religious thought. The New England Town Meeting was about the most distinctly democratic feature in early American life, and that was remarkable for making as little distinction as possible between the secular and the sacred. Men had to come to church. There was an element of compulsion in all religious activities. Men in New England not only had to come to church but had to listen, or at least appear to be listening, while they were there. Distinctive features were the revivals of Whitefield and of Edwards. We read wonderful descriptions of the immensity of the crowds that listened to each of these men, and they were both thoroughly Protestant, and in their day each man creative, in his way. The most famous sermon of Edwards appears to have been "Sinners in the Hands of an Angry God". I have heard religious leaders hold up the preaching of this sermon of Edwards as if it were almost a perfect statement of effective evangelism. We are told that under such preaching conscience-stricken sinners would hold fast to the benches on which they sat to keep from slipping down into a literal hell. If scaring men out of their sins is affirmative and positive preaching, those pioneer preachers performed their task well. Such preaching was not only American but English, for the pulpit of England worked largely by the same or similar methods. George Whitefield was almost, if not quite, as effective in the fields of England as in the open spaces of America. The revivalistic results were largely in emotionalism, and moral changes brought about by emotional results were admirably effective. We may make all the discounts we please about the losses which follow such highly-pitched appeals, and there were heavy losses, but they produced results which deeply influenced ordinary life in their day. Edwards' pictures of hell would seem grotesque to the point of mental aberration if delivered to an audience today, but they were fitted to their time,—especially in America. Probably there has never been more successful religious effort in Protestant history than the preaching of the pioneers. It influenced the after-thought of American theology, ethics, and even the material conquest of the new land. There was plenty of religious debate in those days, much of it quite bitter. I was once pastor of a Methodist church in Ipswich, Massachusetts. There were in my time there, which was over fifty years ago, men and women who had been youngsters when the religious spirit was stirred by a peculiar phenomenon, a contest, if it could be called that, between two mighty preachers of the time, a free-willist Methodist named John Maffitt and Lyman Beecher, spoken of as a predestinationist. One preached to the Methodists, and the other to the Congregationalists. Now, believe it or not, those competitive revivals are, or at least were, mentioned for their effectiveness in the old-church records of the town as remarkable for changed lives, by the acceptance of religious discipleship! The meetings were at the same hour every day for a period of two or three weeks. A very old Methodist, still living at the age of ninety, told me that she met a girl companion after one of Lyman Beecher's sermons who said to her: "Lucy Ann, I was at Dr. Beecher's service last night and was led to indulge a hope." "Indulging a hope is not enough," said Lucy Ann, "you would better come over to the Methodist church and press on till you get the witness of the Spirit."

It would be hard to describe the feelings of even a most worthy church member if he should ever hear two children talking together in such terms today. But "today" is not their day. Their life was grim beyond our understanding. That life had not the manner of the lighter aspects. The serious conquest of a continent was moving on to still more serious stages.

Strange as it may seem to us, even in those days members of different creeds found there was enough of a common devotion to fundamental religious purpose to permit devotees of differing religious fundamentals, as their adherents thought of them, to get together in more or less similar evangelistic effort. Students of religious enterprises throughout the West in the first two decades of the nineteenth century tell us that at the old-time camp-meetings preachers of the most diverse forms of religious belief would preach almost at the same hour from almost adjoining platforms. This is likely a somewhat inaccurate statement, but it does at least hint to us that down under the old-time "Gospel" efforts, there was a grasping after something more vital in religion than talking about it, though such talking is an indisputable first step. Moreover, there was not the immense profusion of subjects and objects of living interest that we have today. My own memory goes back to the period in American community life when opportunities for assembly in large groups, like the meetings of Dwight L. Moody, were both possible and popular, partly for the reason that possibilities of large meetings of any sort were few. Any kind of crowd is interesting, if there are not many crowds.

Making all qualifications like the above, we must see that Protestant religion in its various forms, and they are indeed various, has through the course of American history been a force of positive power. For a long time there has been in this nation a series of attempts to show that American institutions have been chiefly the outcome of economic forces. Attempt has been made through recent years to show that the forces which have shaped American society have been predominantly economic. The power of economic forces in any social life, there is no reason to deny, but it is just as important to ask what purposes are in the minds of the men that run the forces. As important a creative force as any in the thought of our nation today is that as to the constitution of the nation, the spirit in which it was conceived, and the proposed aims of those who founded it in the beginning. The constitution was not an outright, brand-new creation. It voiced and voices principles at which organized humanity had been working for centuries. Those who drafted the document were clearly striving after positive, affirmative results. It is a "Yes" document, putting the seal of the new nation on positive, assertive forces. Professor W. W. Sweet of the University of Chicago is author of a book prepared for publication (1952) entitled, *Religion in the Development of American Culture*. Dr. Sweet writes as follows:

> Numerous studies dealing with the political and economic factors in the making of the [U. S.] Constitution have appeared over the years, but there has been little attention given to the religious influences in the framing and adoption of the fundamental law of the land. The framers of the Constitution represented a cross-section of the American religious bodies of that day. Of them, nineteen were Episcopalians, eight were Congregationalists, seven were Presbyterians, two were Roman Catholics, two were Quakers, one a Methodist, one a Dutch Reformed.

It is true that the Constitution provided that: "No religious test shall ever be required as a qualification to any office or public trust under the United States."

It can hardly be believed that these framers of the Constitution would have been willing to state their religious beliefs if they had been matters of indifference to them. Religious currents were running with powerful force in America in those days. Of course, it is to be expected that economic forces, especially in newly settled lands, move in particular directions, without adequate recognition, but it is rather strained to say that the forces of which men speak earnestly in the foundation of a new state are to be taken as of minor consequence. It does not require any prolonged search in early American archives to discover that preachers like Whitefield, and there were many powerful preachers besides Whitefield, appeared before colonial legislatures and other law-making groups in those far-off days. The positive result of all this was a determining sense of responsibility in law-making. The enactments that public officials were not to be compelled to bind themselves by creedal oaths, did not mean that religion was to be considered of no consequence. It was, indeed, to be taken as of vital consequence, implying that the religious beliefs and activities of men were to be respected as profoundly sacred, and called for freedom in religion.

I have spoken of the preaching of orators like Whitefield as if its high and tense emotionalism lent an atmosphere of unreality to its lofty flights. So it might seem to us if we were to hear it now, but it carried the most profound conviction to those who heard it in Whitefield's day. When Whitefield, preaching to a huge crowd in the midst of a terrific thunderstorm, called out that the flashes and the tumult might be then and there the call to some hearer to an existence in another world, nobody smiled. Hundreds shuddered as if sudden death might be immediately at hand. To doubt in such a spiritual atmosphere would have seemed to scores of hearers like reckless daring in the face of reality, and others might have been thinking they were gazing into the profoundest depths of another world than this. To be sure, the formal philosophy of that day was deistic, but the moral of Whitefield's sermon in a thunderstorm and of the theory of Edwards as to the special nervous system which God provided for the punishment of unrepentant sinners, was not especially deistic. The deist who believed that God had created the world once for all and then had left it to itself, would have had to admit that the non-deists who found ways to make quick returns to human good or bad aspects, certainly had positive effects.

We no sooner state something which seems to say that the religious leaders of the eighteenth century, for example, reached a psychology which appears to us unreal, when we have to add that these men were in the work-a-day, matter-of-fact world amazingly practical.

Benjamin Franklin was in some traits of personal character far away from George Whitefield, on what we today would think of as extreme realism. Yet Franklin admired Whitefield immensely without an indication that he thought of him as in the least insincere. He evidently believed that Whitefield was possessed of altogether extraordinary spiritual powers. Franklin knew that if he himself went to hear Whitefield make an appeal for funds for some worthy cause, that he—Franklin— would throw into the collection box all his available money— a difficulty which Franklin solved by leaving his money at home. Some of Whitefield's biographers have reported that Franklin once went to Whitefield with a proposition to join in an extremely practical enterprise, presumably with a patriotic purpose, so that the enterprise might reap the inestimable financial advantage that the Whitefield oratory would bring to it. This does not mean that Franklin was suggesting any unworthy strategy to Whitefield. Both men believed in the reality of what we might call psychological power, but Franklin, while recognizing its genuineness, would not have placed it in the same category of divinity as did Whitefield. And audiences then probably believed that the Whitefield power came from a higher source than did Franklin.

We are thinking of Protestant religion as affirmative, as resting and issuing from forces indubitably real. Suppose we look for a moment at the strange effect of great human leaders of the later years of the eighteenth century whose religious activities in their working results were among the definitely actual forces of the day. We are thinking especially of Thomas Paine,—or Tom Paine, as he was called over all the known American continent. I wish to refer to Paine's *The Age of Reason*, and his revolutionary career in England, America and France.

I do not think it strange to pronounce Paine's religious service as of positive value, for it gave the more strictly orthodox a hardy opponent some of whose utterances challenged to the utmost the stiffly orthodox theologians of those debating days. The extremely orthodox were lacking in a sense of proportion. Orthodoxy was "all-or-none". The result too often was that a believer accepted rather insignificant details of alleged orthodoxy along with the genuine essentials. Just think of the absurdity which called an openly avowed believer in God and immortality an "atheist". Probably not many theologians of repute did just this, but they did lay such stress on secondary details of Biblical utterance, that they put these details on the same level of importance as God and immortality. One fruitful way of keeping religious thought positive is to keep the teaching centered on truths worth while. Readers of *The Age of Reason* will remember that in one place Paine runs afoul of some defender of a manifest absurdity in the Scriptures on the ground that it was pious "fraud", not that the debater said that, but that was what he meant. Paine replied that such argument is dangerous as "begetting a calamitous necessity of going on." Nobody lays much stress on Paine's theology today, but it had vast importance in its time as giving the orthodox a foeman worthy of their steel. It is maintained by some students of the life of Abraham Lincoln that he was at one period an earnest student of the theology of Tom Paine.

The more important phase of Paine's thinking, however, was in the realm of social, and especially of democratic theory. Even ministers of the gospel who could not endorse Paine's theology could not be prevented from being influenced by his interest in human welfare. The tightness of belief in divine autocracy did not fit well into the vast movements toward the physical conquest of the American West. Nathan Bangs, who wrote about the middle of the nineteenth century a history of the most widely spread religious movements at least as far as the Central West, concedes the influence of the Paine teaching in popular self-government, and this had its consequences for the growth of democratic theory and practice wherever it reached, and it reached through long and wide distances.

Historians are not showing any signs as yet of ceasing to reckon Paine as one of the indispensable revolutionary leaders in three countries—England, America and France. At the period of the revolutions that were stirring in these three nations, England was seeking to arrest Paine, Americans were giving his writings thousands of readers and were thus aiding the leaders of '76. Later, Paine was a figure to be reckoned with during the French Revolution and encountered the eccentric, not to say half-crazy, wrath of Robespierre. He went too far in his democratic passion to suit American heroes like George Washington, but a mental energy like Paine's cannot be left out in any consideration of result-producing forces on the American and European continents. Both in theological and social realms Paine set tongues to talking with a force that has persisted till today. His writings rank with the latest books from students of social fundamentals that are pronounced of current and undying worth. In keeping the church, or the churches, alive to the vital needs of mankind, what we call the human values, Paine cannot be ignored. His significance is all the more inescapable because his mind was trained more in actual human contacts than in libraries. His biographers tell us that in his earlier years he was often to be found speaking to crowds at open-air assemblies in London. He was a disturber of social autocrats in both religious and political circles. He forced issues wherever he appeared. He was always aggressive, and was especially worth while to Protestant teachers of every sort by forcing them to talk about themes worth talking of by living human beings. The writer of these lines passed some of his earliest years in a Central Western community where religious and social circles were always finding time to praise or condemn the theories of Paine. Many writers on American history are to be found implying that aristocratic Americans in high places on this side of the Atlantic, when appealed to for the use of American influence to get Paine out of a prison in Paris, turned a deaf ear, and that it was only James Monroe who found time and resources enough to save him from a death sentence. To keep in mind the theme of this chapter, we may remark that there have been times in human history when the indifference to whether some leader is to be sent to death for his views, is at least a mark of the leader's force in making his views positive and affirmative.

The preaching in this country through the first years of the life of the Republic up to and through the Civil War was marked by deep intensity largely because of the struggles through which the new nation was passing toward adjustment. The relationships both to France and England at the opening of the nineteenth century made for social bitterness, and almost ferocity in public discussion. Had one raised the question with the religious thinkers of those days as to whether their utterances were affirmative, not merely negative, they would hardly have known what the question meant, for each side was desperately in earnest. For one aspect of the struggle was that both sides felt that the contest was almost one of life and death. It is quite a strain for us today to think of Thomas Jefferson as almost an atheist, but that is just about what New Englanders, under the leadership of Timothy Dwight, thought of him, and framed their thought in terms that would hardly be permissible in a pulpit today. Religious and political problems were so intermingled that each seemed a variation on the same theme. French scepticism had large favor with Americans who did not know much about deism, for example, but approved French thought because France had proved so much a friend of Americans during the latter's Revolutionary struggle, and New England could not shake off a preference for the social ideals for which England stood, though without definitely avowing the preference. There followed after a generation of alleged "good feeling" what might be called a lull in such excessive zeal in philosophical and political combat. From that angle of view, the friendship and mutual esteem between Thomas Jefferson and John Adams during their later years, each an ardent philosophical and political leader in his way, can be looked upon as of large significance.

A more desperate conflict was, after the so-called era of good feeling, coming into view on the horizon. This, of course, was the approaching conflict between North and South. There were fundamentally different theories of social organization and of human rights increasingly arising between the two sections, and those differences are asserting themselves vigorously till the present hour, with opposition in changed form but with significance nevertheless. The religious motive was enforced by the conviction on both sides that the slavery question went to the heart of the deeper religious values. In or about the end of the fourth decade, in 1850, a widespread revival broke out both in North and South. When the actual warfare began there were religious leaders both in North and South who were confident that the revivals, which had come almost of themselves, had come to reinforce the forces on whichever side the particular leader happened to be!

The war ended in the exhaustion of one side and the war weariness of the other. Each side believed that the Divine Purpose had favored it, but there has not seemed as much willingness to bring national themes directly into the pulpit as in the days before the war. There has been less willingness to preach on narrowly political questions and more of an attempt to get back to what is called the "old Gospel", except when the corruption of political leaders has become notorious, or national selfishness on one side or the other, or on both sides, has been too evident. There has been a growing sentiment that specific political problems should be discussed mostly under the demands of two-party political organizations. This is at least part of the reason for "keeping politics out of the pulpit", and for making religion more exclusively an individual affair. That usually means that social problems as such are allowed to get along without benefit of clergy, with due allowance for the method of a Henry Ward Beecher, let us say, in this country, and of a Hugh Price Hughes, if we may refer to the English situation as resembling our own.

This lasted well into the latter half of the nineteenth century. It began to dawn on American minds that the individual gospel, so called, had its limitations. The adage that "all guilt is personal" may be good as far as it goes, but it does not go the whole distance. All guilt is personal and may not be individual. Any group of persons is individual in a sense, but a group of individuals may be an organization, working to a merely negative result. Not all the evils of society are the result of evil intents.

Look for an instant at the distribution of offices in a democracy, especially when these are handed out as a reward for political services. In a particular instance this may be innocent enough, or wise enough, but adopted as a regular and accepted practice, it can often just about wreck the individuals of a community by wholesale.

I am not thinking, however, of intentional offenses, but of neglected opportunities which can be used only by corporate action in which the church should take its part. Take the problem of higher education. It was once quite common for church leaders to denounce the churches for the declining effectiveness of the old-time evangelistic efforts. That decline was not by any means the result of a lessening interest but of the fact that the more complex conditions of human living did away with just that type of method. Moreover, we miss sight of the losses of the old-time method. Anyone who has paid attention to the accounts of the mass revivals of our fathers' days remembers the complaints of our fathers at the losses of professing converts. There was not enough gathering up of youth—not enough chance to follow up conversion by careful instruction, not enough chance to set the Christian experience to work. If the churches had had only the Gospel to preach, the calling sinners away from their sins, and not equal opportunity to practice the doing of good, the churches would be in a dubious position today.

Or take the church in the success it won in bringing a religious atmosphere into education. It is easy enough for us today, living in the midst of the most elaborate educational equipment any nation has ever known, at least on the material side, to forget the genuinely constructive work done by the churches in the last century and a half. The start for popular education in this nation was in almost every case made by the churches, or at least under church auspices or influences. There was, of course, a lack of scientific equipment, even in the days which some of us can easily remember, but that was in part met by the religious ideals of the human values which strictly scientific methods are not always careful to guard. Within the period of my own recollection, one of the foremost universities in America offered only one course in what it was pleased to call philosophy, and that was in Haeckel's *Riddles of the Universe*. The reason for this was that the institution was fearful that the university might lose standing by being thought of as yielding to a religious demand in a nation which was supposed not to have in education any one religious system as over against any other. We may well be thankful that we have come upon better days, but even now the churches are finding a way of supplementing the technical scientific instruction by religious foundations at the seats of the state universities without being under the control of the institutions, and yet in harmony with the general educational aims. If there is any more important, more positive task in which the churches are working just now, it would be hard to tell what it is.

Moreover, we must not forget the greatness of the importance of the actual foreign missionary work being carried forward in almost all lands, if not quite all. In many a land the only hope for anything beyond the mere routine of staying alive is due to the most pronounced help of the Christian missionary. There is nothing to eat beyond the barest necessities. The missionary has nothing to contribute in actual material, but instruction as to how to make the earth, or man's toil upon the earth, bring larger and better returns; this dependent upon teaching a larger worth in a man's life, a new dignity and a new hope. The support of Protestantism to missionary effort in non-Christian lands, pitifully inadequate though it is, is the most hopeful prospect for a truer building up of mankind now to be seen in the relations between the so-called more-favored and the less-favored peoples. The most constructive force that can be turned on men anywhere is the power that reveals them to themselves with an opportunity that sets that force to work. For the sake of its own salvation, the civilized world, so-called, will have soon to set itself to preserve itself from actual physical destruction. The most effective preservative forces are those of moral purpose, and the highest form of that purpose takes the noblest forces of Christianity to preach the use of that power to make and keep the world safe not merely for democracy as an organization, but for human beings as such, teaching them to bring out the best in themselves by helping one another. This all sounds commonplace, but the mightiest forces in nature are now coming into full view as the deadliest the world has ever seen. From the positive side, the greatest contribution to civilization the forces of Christianity could make would be the creation of a world-wide sentiment that would demand the use of atomic energy for the benefit of humanity. The world as a whole has not yet reached the stage where it could be trusted to have such powers put in its hands. National sentiment, taking all the nations together, has not yet brought such destructive forces under moral control as to be trusted to use them for constructive ends. Indeed, any single nation coming now to such control would find it all too easy to think of itself as warranted in putting other nations out of the way. Any such nation might be so scared by the presence of evils of one sort or another as to think itself warranted to put all such evils out of the path of civilization by force,—and it requires the highest moral character to use force for destructive purposes at all.

Here we reach the most baffling problem of all large-scale progress. The temptation on the part of a self-righteous civilization, honest enough under modern social conditions, to think of itself as called to put the whole world in order, and thus might soon destroy the world as effectively as our world's falling into the sun, if we could imagine such an astronomical catastrophe. Our world has not yet reached the stage of true moral development to enable us to think of unlimited national power in morally limited human hands without frantic nightmare.

On the whole, the development of political forces in so-called democratic nations needs a new more vigorous insistence on the older doctrines than that it is now receiving, or on some applications that carry on their spirit. Here we must keep in mind the danger that comes with the impressiveness of bigness. Just at present we are all experiencing the thrill from the welcome tendencies toward the ecumenical in Protestantism. Up to date, these tendencies are among the most healthy that Protestantism has known, but already we are beginning to hear that the most forward-looking groups must be careful in their advocacy of the more radical social opinions. There must, however, be room for the consideration of a more radical Christianity than we have yet known. We need not be Communists to call for a more thoroughgoing social adaptation of Christianity to modern life than we have yet tried. We need have no hesitation in protesting against the degradation of the mind and soul of man by Russian ideologies, and we must be thankful for as much humanization of material forces as we already have, but we are far, far yet from the Christian conversion and sanctification of such forces.

I repeat that this calls for large liberty for utterance even if we come to one Protestant body. Indeed, if such provision is not made, the progress of that body will be slow indeed, and may finally come in some militaristic form. In some directions the churches have already attained to moral liberty. In almost all denominations some forms of progress—I refer especially to political programs put before the public by vote—result in discussion by church members, without undue bitterness between members of opposing political parties, a result which is immensely to the good, but this is not attained without previous thought and discussion by pioneers who wish to make their Christianity count.

We say, "Like a mighty army moves the Church of God." Not just yet! Beginning! Not till millions have talked and talked and talked,—for this talking, in spite of all its commonplaceness, makes the atmosphere in which the genuinely constructive gets its chance.

SUGGESTIONS FOR FURTHER READING

GEORGE M. STEPHENSON, *The Puritan Heritage* (New York, 1952).

W. W. SWEET, *Religion in the Development of American Culture* (New York, 1952).

J. PAUL WILLIAMS, *What Americans Believe and How They Worship* (New York, 1952).

W. E. GARRISON, *A Protestant Manifesto* (Nashville, 1951).

THE CREDO OF AN UNREGENERATE LIBERAL

By
MORTON SCOTT ENSLIN

MORTON SCOTT ENSLIN

Since 1924 Professor Enslin has been a member of the faculty of Crozer Theological Seminary in Chester, Pennsylvania. He is widely known as one of the foremost scholars in the field of early Christianity, two of his books, "The Ethics of Paul" (1930) and "Christian Beginnings" (1938) having acquired the deserved reputation of being among the most widely used texts in this field. Favorably known for many years as editor of one of America's most significant theological journals, the "Crozer Quarterly", his voice has been heard across the land as an outspoken defender of a vigorously liberal conception of the Christian religion. An earned Doctor of Theology of Harvard and an honorary Doctor of Divinity of Colby College, Professor Enslin has held posts of leadership in such academic fraternities as the American Theological Society (president, 1952), the Society of Biblical Literature and Exegesis (president, 1945), American Oriental Society as well as other groups. He has been a visiting lecturer of patristics in the Graduate School of the University of Pennsylvania since 1926. He is heard gladly as a visiting preacher at Harvard and other colleges and as a lecturer. His style of presentation is striking, his thoughts unmistakable when set forth either orally or in writing and his opinions come from an honest and well informed mind. An essay on Protestantism out of his long reflections carries weight and should stir any reader from an easy going complacency of mere acceptance of frozen beliefs and habit patterns.

Editor

THE CREDO OF AN UNREGENERATE LIBERAL

Morton Scott Enslin

THE CHARGE is often made that the Protestant, more especially the liberal Protestant, believes nothing. He may belong nominally to a communion in which the repetition of some creed, the so-called Apostles' Creed or the Nicene Creed, is a normal part of the service of worship, and he may even repeat it from week to week; but to a large extent his repetition of it is mechanical and of a piece with his attitude in singing many of the hymns. These too he joins in, but his singing proves nothing. They are part of a familiar and accustomed service. But so far as believing the various sentiments expressed, that is a quite different matter.

This charge has long been made by the fundamentalists, both within Protestantism and without. The liberal may be an estimable man—or, to use the phrase beloved by many who make this charge, may be a "good moral man"—but he is definitely not a Christian and should in simple honesty cease pretending so to be. His failure to accept the pronouncement of those who speak with authority—be they the self-appointed custodians of a Book which they profess to believe from cover to cover, or the divinely appointed successors of the Apostles with a complete and authoritative tradition—makes him suspect. They have the truth, divinely bestowed upon them; since he does not appear to believe what they do, or think they do, he believes nothing.

More recently this ancient chorus has been augmented by another choir, largely recruited from within liberalism itself, who are insisting that liberal theology has demonstrated its own bankruptcy. Its unconcern with doctrine, its insistence on tolerance—"live and let live"—must give way to a new orthodoxy, an insistence on the central place of a real and authoritative theology, God-given and the only integrating force in all history.

At this time when so many funeral sermons are being preached over the late and not too widely lamented liberalism which has finally died because of its lack of affirmative belief, it may be properly asked if the preachers are not a bit premature in their committal services. Is the corpse really as dead as it is confidently asserted? To many of us, the answer is a definite and decided No. It is true that liberalism in many theological quarters is weakening; not because there are fewer liberals nor because they have grown feeble and moribund through lack of belief, but because the liberal spirit of search and quest is offended and repulsed, even disgusted, at the reactionary trend of so much purported theology rampant today—the arrogant and self-satisfied Roman Catholic Church with its rigid and uncompromising hatred of freedom and all which that term entails; the fundamentalist with his vulgar and noisy championing of a book which he tends to make cheap and unlovely, if not suspect, by his own intolerance; the new wave of neoörthodoxy which appears hardly more than a new crop of fundamentalists with faces washed, hair combed, and dressed in evening clothes. There are plenty of liberals in every field except theology. They are being driven away from religion, in part by the self-designated purveyors of the "gospel once for all delivered to the saints" who appear to them to deny in religion all those attitudes of mind which they have been trained to prize everywhere else, in part by the irrationalism of the theologians themselves. It seems to them that to attend a service of worship—for too often they fail to realize that the noisy champions of pure religion undefiled are often not the only ones who are religious—they must park their brains along with their automobiles at the curb outside, and this they properly refuse to do. They hear that there is a great increase in church attendance in recent months, read the rosy reports of the evidence disclosed by church censuses, and not unnaturally are inclined to accept the contention of the advocates of the new orthodoxy that this new wave of interest in religion is the natural fruit of a tree made once more fertile by "faith" in an altogether other God with imperious and irrational demands upon a hopelessly impotent and doomed humanity. This but adds to the conviction of many a liberal that he had been right all along in feeling that religion and its church were no place for him. It is not that he is not interested in finding answers to his queries; it is simply that these purported answers do not seem to him answers at all.

Thus not only to the easy and unwarranted contention that liberalism is dead but to the companion charge that the liberal does not believe anything an unqualified and emphatic No is to be registered. The liberal believes many things and believes them with an intensity that often terrifies him. He may well be suspicious of what his critics style "faith". To him it often seems that as commonly bandied about "faith" means believing a thing in lieu of evidence, more often, in spite of distinct evidence to the contrary; that is, it is a blind and obstinate belief that things happened in the past and will in the future, which his training has led him to be convinced are impossible and of a nature to negate what he knows to be true. He has heard so often that for the real Christian faith is the quality which is evidenced by the doughty churchman of the yesteryears: *Credo quia absurdum.* That appears to him, however impressively it may be intoned, as pigheaded and obstinate credulity and no solid foundation on which to build. Thus he turns away in suspicion from the insistence, so widespread at the moment, that God's "plan for salvation", which he is being told is writ large in the Bible when the latter book is read aright—not as willful and captious critics would have it read: "piecemeal"; but as one consistent and connected account of an event long prophesied and finally realized and which really makes all subsequent history definitely anticlimactic, if not actually meaningless—is admittedly contrary to reason and cannot be supported by factual proofs. Instead it must be accepted on faith, must be believed without evidence and even despite evidence. Then, if he has faith, really believes it, he will eventually see the evidence for it.

This is to him too high a price to pay. His experience in other realms of thought and training points in the precisely opposite direction. He has been trained to let his findings determine his feelings, that is, constitute his faith; he is most unwilling to put the cart before the horse and let his feelings determine what he is to find. Such faith, he properly insists, is simply credulity. Thus he is styled a man of "little faith". But let him define the word faith himself, and the situation is very different. For him faith is not so much a system or congeries of beliefs, be they good, bad, or indifferent. Rather it is a quality of life; more than that, it is a quality of life which scorns consequences.

Thus the real problem for the religious liberal, the genuine modern Protestant, is one which has been in essence present from the very beginning of the Christian movement but which has been rendered very acute in recent years. It is the problem of an historic religion which has from the beginning believed itself to be a revealed religion; that is, that at a moment—or series of them—God revealed to man his will and purpose. As stated in these terms, and without additions, the situation might not seem so acute. There are, however, additions, and these are the elements which cause the difficulty.

Christianity's origin was in a world utterly and entirely different from the one we live in. It is not merely that the formative days are nineteen hundred years removed; at some times in the developing story we call history changes have been very slow, and two thousand years have been less a remove than one hundred at a different stage. This is not the case today. The last three centuries have passed at a rapid tempo. Hence today the problem is singularly acute. We live in a world which has been separated from the past by a gulf comparatively modern in origin, which simply can't be bridged.

[76]

THE CREDO OF AN UNREGENERATE LIBERAL

At the time when Christianity came into existence—to use a not too happy but probably understandable compression of speech—the world was believed to be solitary and unique. It was not a tiny bit torn from a larger body, the latter also literally but microscopic in the vast encompassing universe, as today every child knows it to be. Instead, it was, so to speak, the universe. The sun and moon and stars were simply lights fashioned by a benevolent God to illumine his *chef d'oeuvre* by day and by night. This earth was flat, was stationary. Somewhere above it was heaven, where God and his angels dwelled and to which in the future the fortunate would be removed. Beneath it was the place of punishment, to which sinners would eventually be consigned.

God was essentially a big man. Some early Christians might have shied away from the term, but it is idle to deny that the language used to describe him was of a nature to make virtual anthropomorphizing of him, despite theological statements, inevitable. There were no immutable laws. Gravity was unknown. Stones fell down, not up, because God willed them so to do. The sun moved across the heavens for the same reason. If God chose to alter that arrangement—as he occasionally did, as in the case of his friend Joshua—he could do so. Not infrequently he intervened, to aid his friends, punish his enemies. Prayer in the form of petition was perfectly natural and proper. So were various other forms of magic with which his especial friends were on occasion especially endowed.

Some today may object to this as an oversimplification and somewhat crass description if not an actual burlesque. It may for the moment shock some of the overtender as a ruthless stripping of the ornaments from the cosmic Christmas tree. Sober reflection will probably convince most that it is not in violence of the facts.

We do not today live in that sort of world. During the last four hundred years one door after another has been unlocked, many windows have been opened. The results have been beyond any compare. Never before in the history of life on this little planet has there been a period really commensurate, and just now are we gradually becoming aware of its consequences.

The foundations of the Christian religion, historically speaking, were laid in that other world: our views of God, man, the future—in a word, the stuff of theology. God had revealed to man, in a book which in actual fact he had himself composed although he had chosen to use various figures divinely inspired as, so to speak, amanuenses, all that man would ever need to know to find himself in perfect relations both with his fellows and his creator. Our religious terminology stems from this earlier world in which no one of us could possibly find himself at home. The very titles of God—Father, Creator—hallowed to us by centuries of use, make it very difficult for all save a few to avoid what is frequently dubbed a very material view of God. If God made man in his own image, it is not surprising if the rank and file of men should continue to assume that since men look like God, God must in turn look like a man. Many, of course, have tried to reëvaluate that type of thinking. It is to be doubted with what real success. We may continue to call God "Father", to address him as "Thou", to describe him in terms of what to us are the most valued and longed for qualities. How long thinking men will be able to continue these adjustments in thought is to me far from clear.

This is but one phase—to me it is a fair and illustrative one—of the problem which the liberal Protestant faces today. Can he continue to live in two worlds at the same time, to perform a constant and unending translation of terms of the one into realities of the other? It is because an increasingly large number of men and women cannot and are even ceasing to try that the traditionalists seem to have justice in their contention that this is an age of unbelief; that liberals do not believe anything. I, for one, am inclined to state perfectly clearly, and without apology, that for me personally it is sheer impossibility to affirm beliefs in many of the things which those of the first century accepted without question. I am inclined to add, and not as a wisecrack, that I am convinced that were many of them—to be specific, Jesus of Nazareth and Paul of Tarsus—to be alive in twentieth-century America, their views and expressions would be vastly different from what is recorded about them in Holy Writ.

Now despite the contentions of many fundamentalists, Christianity is not simply the unchanged, undeveloped, carry-over of first-century Palestinian thought. To be sure, there is still the unctuous plea that we "go back to Jesus". To the liberal it is stupid and meaningless. It sounds as if it were a warm and honest reaffirmation of values perennially discovered in that radiant figure of the past. Actually it is nothing of the sort. In short, it is a crass and iconoclastic denial of all the subsequent values and insights. It is, in a word, the rejection of Paul and of all the other figures who have brought their contributions—preachers may prefer to style it their "gold, and frankincense, and myrrh".

This must be frankly faced. Christianity is not, and never has been, a stagnant pool. Rather it has been from its very first a river fed by innumerable tributaries and streams, flowing constantly onward. Traditionalists may continue to style it "the faith once for all delivered to the saints" or to describe it, in part or in whole, as *"semper, ubique, et ab omnibus."* No one who knows its history will be inclined so to do, nor will he feel any loss in not so doing. To him it seems as absurd as would the act of a man standing near the mouth of the Mississippi and denying that this vast stream *is* the Mississippi, insisting that only the water in it that came from the Lake of the Woods is genuine and usable.

Thus it appears to me long overdue for the liberal in religion to realize that there is no need for him to try to live in the yesterdays of his religion. He does not speak Aramaic or wear garments of the sort worn in first-century Palestine—or even in Corinth or Rome. I can see no reason for him to strive to think or express himself like a man in the first century.

In the same breath I would add: He should be equally unwilling to attempt to make those who lived in the first century put on garments and embrace ideas to which he in the twentieth century is accustomed. He may be greatly interested in the early days of our historic religion. I cannot see how he can refrain from interest in them—and no idle curiosity either. He feels himself but one in a long line of men and women struggling on to the far horizon; there is no reason for him to seek to modernize his predecessors or to archaize himself.

Among the reasons for the charge that the liberal Protestant does not "believe anything in particular" is his view of the Bible. Here the charge is specific and pointed: "He does not believe in the dear old Book." The charge is stupid, uninformed, and frequently malicious. If honestly believed, it would be put: "He does not believe what I believe about it." To the liberal the Bible is not what it was in the eyes of the first-century Jew or Christian. For them it was the complete, entire, and all-embracing revelation of God in which was contained God's complete and entire will for mankind. It was unlike any other book, was written literally by God, not by any man or men, and, while a complete picture of the past, was more than that, in that it was the blueprint for the future as well. Thus everything that men needed to know was there; everything that was ever to happen was depicted. It was all there, but it was implicit, was, so to speak, written in invisible ink; it must be made explicit. But not only could that be done; it must be done, and it was done.

To the liberal the Bible is not this. Instead it is something far more. Rather it is the record of centuries of achievement and pilgrimage of men and women like himself confronted with the tasks and problems of life. In the course of the years they made many discoveries, gained many insights. It is to him a priceless heritage of the past, and in it he finds much that aids him in his constant search for the gold of life. He is not in the slightest surprised to find it not infrequently self-contradictory were it to be regarded as one book. He knows that it is nothing of the sort but rather a library written by many men over the period of a thousand years. He is not surprised at differences and contradictory points of view. He sees great differences between the God who encouraged Abraham to lie to his host regarding the status of Sarah, who caused Samuel to hew Agag to pieces, and who apparently approved of Samson and Esther, and the God of the prophets and Jesus. He is not surprised at the naïve explanation of the fashioning of the world and its occupants, of the deluge and its contradictory accounts, and is inclined to smile when the name of Ingersoll is mentioned and his famous *Some Mistakes of Moses*. He is aware that before his eyes is revealed much that is cruel and trivial and perverse, much that is noble and lofty and of the sort that makes his heart glow within him with the hope that he can make in his day a contribution akin to those which some of his forebears made in theirs.

Thus of course he welcomes the work of honest and devoted scholars who through the years have sought to unlock this legacy of the past. To him it is a book to be read and appreciated. The more light shed on its pages the happier he is. And he is not afraid that the light will in the slightest degree injure the volume he finds of increasing worth. When he is challenged by the brash, "So you don't believe the Bible," he is inclined, after perhaps a moment of annoyance at what appears to him bad manners and poor taste, to answer: "I love it, and that seems to me vastly more important."

He reads the story of Jesus and wishes he knew more about him. One thing stands out very clear. Here was a man who had an amazing quality of inspiring, convincing, nerving men and women to a confidence that nothing could shake, and who sent them out as purveyors of a new gospel of hope and confidence which brought strength to the nerveless hands and feeble knees of men and women discouraged, disillusioned, enmeshed in a veritable failure of nerve. And it seems to him perfectly natural that in the course of the years there should have come to be attributed to Jesus many sayings and doings which the camera and notebook of a first-century reporter might well have failed to include. He feels himself fortunate that he is in a heritage which has for its central figure one such that to each succeeding generation it has seemed natural and appropriate to find in him the embodiment and earnest of its own highest dreams and wistful longings. He is thus not surprised nor particularly concerned when he discovers that apparently this individual who lived in the first century thought and acted as one in the first century; that he was talking to those of his own day, not to us over their heads. If it seems to him probable that Jesus believed that the world was speedily to come to an end—as most certainly his early followers and their successors did—it will not in the least disturb him. The thing that would surprise him would be to discover that Jesus knew and talked about atomic fission. On the other hand, he will neither try to manipulate the records so as to free Jesus from his notions nor will he himself be in the slightest degree inclined to adopt such a view as his own to-day. He is quite content to let one who was the child of the first century live in the first century. He will prize many of his insights which seem so thoroughly to have withstood the ravages of time, and his constant prayer will be that he may be as loyal and honest in meeting his problems in twentieth-century America as was Jesus his very different ones in Galilee and Jerusalem nineteen hundred years ago.

Such questions as the virgin birth, miracles of healing or over nature, or the reality of a bodily resurrection and resultant empty tomb, which were of tremendous concern to an earlier generation, will not loom large or seem of much importance. Familiar with other religions and cultures, he will find it increasingly difficult to regard such stories in one culture as essentially different from those told of other heroes in parallel or earlier cultures. He will be inclined to regard them in terms of poetry rather than of factual history, to see them as evaluations of a later day as men sought to explain in terms and categories natural to them their appreciation and regard for one whose deathless influence continued unabated. Titles such as *Lord, Christ, Messiah, Only Begotten Son, Son of David, Son of Man, Son of God,* will be seen in their natural and original setting. Questions such as: Were his teachings unique? Was he sinless? Did his physical death on Golgotha actually and in a manner distinct and different in kind achieve our salvation?—will probably not loom nearly so large as during earlier generations and, in all likelihood, will prove of decreasing importance with the passing of the years. He will continue to read and appreciate the stories of the one whose deathless influence has become increasingly great through the years, not only upon those who came into personal contact with him but upon all subsequent generations. And he will welcome all the help he can obtain which tends to throw light upon what is at once an enigma and a challenge. He may well ponder the saying of old with increasing insight: "Thou shalt call his name Jesus, for he shall save his people from their sins." It is likely that he will feel increasingly certain that men of a former day greatly erred in understanding those words to mean "save them from the consequence of their sins," for he knows the impossibility of that in an honest universe. It may well seem to him, as he reads and rereads that tragically lovely story of the years, with insight quickened as he sees it so often repeated, that here we have a blueprint of life, the tragedy that is so constantly recurring, the deadly costliness of sin and ignorance, of bigotry and intolerance, which so regularly send the innocent and the guiltless to their doom. And seeing it, he finds himself strengthened in his resolve that his shall not be the hands which drive the nails.

Thus problems and queries which caused endless and often furious debate through earlier centuries, such as original sin, the fall of man, atonement, even salvation, will not appear to him of great practical importance. He will be interested in them, especially if history exerts for him a fascination; but they will seem to him definitely dated, the effort of men to grapple with and solve problems which while of prime importance to them have gradually retreated from the centre of the scene today.

He will not shy away from the word sin; instead he will be quite aware of its presence. He may be less certain of its precise nature. At times he will be inclined to wonder whether it is the deliberate and determined refusal to do what the man knows he should do: the defiant "I won't" to the clear command, "Go, work in the vineyard". It may well seem to him that the ancient Greeks were right in their insistence that failure to hit the mark was essentially due to ignorance; that if the man could see what was right, he would do it. He will labor under no delusion that this lightens the load or makes the remedy more easy. Sometimes the man's mental eyes are so shortsighted, so affected with moral astigmatism that a veritable operation is necessary. Thus he will never close the door to what is styled conversion or rebirth. He will know that it is a reality, for he will have seen it in fact, may conceivably have felt it in himself. But this will not cause him to feel that it is the only solution. In many cases such a radical cure is utterly unnecessary and its diagnosis pathological. Because there are some men who seem blind to the values of life, some who, like the prodigal of old, have rebelliously gone off to the far country, he will not regard all his friends and neighbors either as prodigals or cases for pathological probing preparatory to spiritual surgery. He will be far more concerned in using his influence and talents in averting by anticipation the tragedies which lead to the sojourn in the far country, for he will consider each such shipwreck a failure of the society of which he is a part. And he will not feel easy in blaming Adam for what he is acutely aware lies far nearer his own home.

As a liberal he will be increasingly suspicious of the constant attempt to minimize and lessen the dignity of man. That there are evil men he will be well aware, and he will well know that they will be repaid, and bitterly, for their evil, for the universe in which we live is an honest one, in which rewards and penalties come with amazing regularity. He will deplore the artificial and abysmal cleavage which, it seems to him, some theologians are delighting to make between a perfect God and utterly helpless and hopeless men. This contrast will seem to him not only wrong but wrongheaded, and it will seem to him to run counter to the facts of life as he observes them. The insistence upon man's inability, his helplessness, his passive and fettered state until an altogether other God deigns or condescends to reach down and make alive what was inert and blind, appears to him perverse and vicious. He may even wish, as he reads the elaborate and wordy discussion of this oft-asserted utter separation between the Creator and the created which modern prophets of despair seem so delighted to dwell upon, that they might complete the verse which they seem so regularly to choose as their text: "God is in heaven, and thou upon earth." He will remember, as they seem so often to forget, that the concluding words of that gentle critic from the past were "therefore let thy words be few."

So many are the cases of amazing courage, of lovely devotion, of understanding and genuine self-sacrifice, of integrity, insight, and tireless love which he can see on every hand, when he takes the trouble to look, that the windy blasts of the prophets of total depravity and universal helplessness seem to him both noxious and often blasphemous. In the light of what his eyes see, when he is content to use them instead of sitting back conjuring up what he ought to see, he will not be unduly surprised when a foot slips, his own or one of those with whom he rubs shoulders; nor will it blind his eyes to the many which stand firm and solid.

Even more important—perhaps better said, more fundamental, and thus in itself the explanation for the other—he will find himself increasingly unconcerned with the age-long debate as to whether this is or is not a friendly universe in which we live, a term which he may well prefer to the query more common in theological circles: Are we the creatures of a friendly God? It will seem to him that this is one of those useless and pointless questions which can be easily raised but for which a convincing answer is impossible, save to those already convinced.

He sees perfectly clearly that for every case or example proffered in support of the affirmative position an equally clear-cut example suggesting the reverse can be countered. The sea gull on the head of the starving flyer in the mid Pacific, the bullet deflected by a pocket testament and a mother's prayer at home, the patient miraculously cured of an altogether fatal disease—these may be momentarily impressive to those who have experienced them; but what about the thousands who went to their deaths without the friendly intervention from above, the many felled by bullets or bayonets despite their faith and their mothers' prayers, the fairy daughter torn from agonized parents by the dread disease? And when, if he is very young, he counters with these cases in the course of the debate, the answer he receives will not likely seem to him impressive.

It appears to him—at least it does to me—that in the future this sort of logomachy, which leads inevitably to such sorry and lamentable escapes as styling as "acts of God" all the hellish calamities for which no human being or adequate cause can be found, will prove of decreasing concern to intelligent men and women. To the liberal, instead of this endless and pointless argument another question will seem pointed: "Are we friendly to the universe?" When that question is raised and honestly answered, we find ourselves on solid ground. The world may be hard, but it is honest. Results succeed causes with amazing regularity. Wheat when sown produces more wheat, not barley. And if the farmer makes a mistake because of the darkness of his barn or the confusion in his own head and picks up and sows the wrong seed, his regrets and his prayers will not affect the crop. For the lazy and the careless that is tragedy. To the honest workman it is the source of the greatest confidence and security.

Is a buzz saw friendly? No one thinks of asking the question. But if one uses the buzz saw with sobriety and skill, he finds it will cut his wood most expeditiously. If he proves careless or clumsy, he will likely find that it will take off his hand or arm as expeditiously as it cuts the log. The liberal may well see in this a parable of life. Iron and coal are in the earth for the taking. What the miner and manufacturer will do with them must be answered by the latter. The iron is equally available to form rails and Diesels for the transportation of goods and riders, to frame schools and hospitals, or for the production of guns and bullets. The chemicals are equally ready to the hand of the doctor and the murderer. Strychnine in the hands of the skilled physician will keep a tired heart ticking; in the hands of the murderer will stop the heart forever.

To some this seeming unconcern of Nature—her winds will drive ships, turn windmills, or level houses and dash ships on lee shores; her fires will heat, produce power, wipe out forests and level cities—to some this seeming unconcern is more terrible and deadly than an open and avowed hostility. To the liberal it does not seem so. Instead it is a constant source of satisfaction and confidence. Instead of caprice and chance we have regularity and order. Nature may be a hard and demanding mistress. She surely plays no favorites, sparing her friends and blasting her enemies. When a man obeys her laws, he finds her friendly; if he proves careless and unconcerned, he pays the price for his folly. She does not obtrude her values. They must be searched for. But honest search is rewarded; careless and willful disregard is punished.

Thus it seems to many a liberal that while we may be inclined to continue hallowed phrases, we must put into them so substantially new a content that eventually a change in nomenclature is well-nigh certain. At times he regrets this, for he is not recklessly iconoclastic, however often that charge is made. He labors under no delusion that all that is new is good any more than he does that its companion, all that is good is new, is true. But at times he feels that he must make a definite break with the past. He reads with interest the reported word of the one whose name is dear about the folly of putting new wine into old skins; and he finds no little satisfaction in the fact that that one did not, on that account, deplore the use of the new wine; that instead he advised putting it into new and presumably stronger, less brittle, containers.

He sees what appear to him examples of this wise counsel on every hand. It seems to him that many of the views which are commonly stressed as essential to the Christian faith are such as would never have been devised by man like himself with a reasonable knowledge of what is written large in the face of the earth and in the stars above him. He cannot in simple honesty, even if he would, blind his eyes and deafen his ears to what appear to him certain, definite, and of a sort demonstrable by honest tests. Thus to him such terms and notions as heaven and hell, salvation achieved once and for all through the death of one innocent of wrong and then transferred by a sort of dubious cosmic bookkeeping to the credit of the guilty, a future final judgment, not to mention a second coming of the Lord Jesus, descending in bodily form from a heaven which can no longer be regarded as "up" to a world no longer flat and motionless but spherical and whirling on its axis, are of little consequence if not downright meaningless, although for men of a different age who had wrought them from their own heritage and experience they were all-important. He may continue to use them, because they have become hallowed with the years, but he will interpret them in a way different from what their first champions intended.

And he will do it with no sense of guilt or dishonesty. To the charge that he is untrue or perverse toward the timeless revelation of God, he will be quite undisturbed. What he knows, or thinks that he knows, about this universe in which he lives leads him to think that "revelation" as commonly bandied about is another one of those terms from the past which once had meaning but has now lost its essential usefulness. He breaks entirely with the ancient view which saw particular men as mouthpieces of the Eternal, repeating, essentially parrotwise, what was supernaturally put into their mouths to speak. He does not reject their message on that ground. Rather he tests it. At times it seems to him that they had profound and unerring insights which still have tremendous significance when translated into modern speech. These he prizes, not so much because Isaiah or Amos, Jesus or Paul, said them, as because they still have point and compelling power. What he denies is the notion that such insights were "revealed." To him they seem discovery, experience, the result of search, of testing, of trial and error. He may even continue to use such conventional phrases as "God says" or "God thinks", but he will have no delusion as to *how* God says and thinks; to him the story of the years makes very clear that what God has said and thought and done he has said and thought and done through human heads and hearts and mouths.

Thus he is particularly cold toward terms and phrases cast in the form of timeless absolutes. Elatives he understands and appreciates; uncompromising superlatives he finds alien to his thinking. In the poetry of religion he may accept with appreciation such a term as "Only Begotten Son," as a natural and appropriate declaration of recognized worth. When intended in a literal sense, as isolating or making unique or final this figure of the distant past, the term seems to him both meaningless and unwarranted. To him nothing is final. That smacks of the stagnant pool, not the onflowing river.

To the notion that within history there is special chapter to be regarded as "holy history", that in the distant past the decisive battle of the cosmic war was waged and won, and that all subsequent events are simply reflections, consequences

[89]

of that one all-important event, just as all previous events had been preliminary to, if not actually predictive of, that cosmic watershed, he cannot subscribe. On the contrary, to him every age has been of profound and real significance in the developing pattern he knows as life. Events do not just happen. They always have causes, and in turn they are in themselves causes for what is still to be. Thus there can be, in any real sense, no "dark ages". At times events may seem to have moved now more rapidly, now more slowly; men may seem now more, now less fertile and gifted with insight; but all have played their part. Without them the present day would have been far different.

To the charge that he has moved a long way from the position occupied by his fellow Christians, not alone of the first and second centuries but of the fifteenth he will assent, and with no embarrassment. If to be Christian means, as some noisily insist, to live in the past, to close one's eyes to the present and its patent teachings, he must relinquish the title. But this he is by no means inclined to do. To be a "follower of Jesus" does not mean to him to ape the ways of Jesus, to think his thoughts; rather it means to meet his tasks, attempt to solve his problems, to carry his load with the same devotion and spirit of integrity as did this predecessor. At times it even seems to him that he has a greater appreciation for him, stands in greater and more wistful awe of him, than do many of his contemporaries who apparently find their attention turned almost exclusively to the portents wrought upon him at the times of his conception and death, as the real elements of value and proof of divine greatness.

At the charge brought against Protestants in general of divisiveness, of having proved false to the divine imperative: "That they be one", he is not particularly impressed. That there are too many branches and twigs on the Protestant tree he will readily agree. That in comparison with the efficiency of a highly organized body like the Roman Catholic Church, ideally geared for power politics, Protestantism is greatly inefficient he knows equally well. But to him that has its compensations. Democracy, he ruefully knows, is by its very essence inefficient; it seems again and again as if it moves two steps up and not one but three back. Nonetheless he is a confirmed and unrepentant democrat. Though he deplores the cantankerous and narrow bigotry so evident in many of the rival sects, great and small alike, and welcomes every sign of these being lessened and decreased, he is not overenthusiastic about the prospects of the "one great Protestant Church" just around the corner, at least as most of its present artists paint it. Understanding, mutual respect, intelligent coöperation—these he applauds and considers essential; and, if he be intellectually honest, he is not satisfied with approving in theory, but is actively engaged in bringing them to pass, for to him "faith without works" is one phrase from the distant past which needs never be suspect. Corporate union, the creation of one great uniform Protestant superchurch— that is quite another matter. Aside from many practical problems which appear to him very real is the still greater danger: Would not such a creation prove a veritable Frankenstein? Have not the rights of minorities been safeguarded and made sacred in direct consequence of the fortunate absence of one great superchurch? This gives him pause. He is unwilling to see the upset and overthrow of what he is convinced is one of the greatest blessings and achievements this planet has ever seen.

He finds profound values in the church, as made up of hundreds and thousands of local groups in which men and women work together for the realization of some of their dearest hopes and longings. He is little inclined to argue about its precise nature. Such terms as "divine institution", "invisible body of the elect", may even appear to him not only dated but largely meaningless. He gladly recognizes the profound influence for what he regards of distinct value that these groups have exerted through the years, and he feels himself proud and happy to be associated with his fellows in a companionship and fellowship that is singularly effective in multiplying the strength of individual achievement. And he wishes devoutly for better leadership.

Worship, the appreciation of values present on every hand but often overlooked because of their nearness and frequency —these are real to him, and he finds it congenial to associate with his fellows in this common quest. That he is more holy while in church than when engaged in the daily course of life may seem to him doubtful. He is nonetheless aware that it is wholesome and altogether necessary at times to catch one's breath, to take stock of life, to plan and to appraise.

When these elements are to the fore in a service of worship, he finds them of priceless value, and he leaves with the feeling that it has been good for him to be there. Into some of the elements common to the service he may well see fit to pour his own values. Probably prayer is to many a liberal Protestant one such. The incoherent and tasteless barrage of petition for especial favors which often go by the name of prayer leaves him cold. This smacks of magic and in his world magic and witchcraft have no place. Gratitude for blessings very real which have been his, meditation in which he seeks ways to straighten out some of the tangles in which he finds his feet caught, aspiration in which he envisions to himself, and in which he can join with his fellows in common phrase, the desired goals he hopes to achieve—these are to him of value, and he prizes the opportunities to give them greater growth.

So far as the sacraments, or as many Protestants prefer to style them, the ordinances, are concerned, the liberal Protestant again will likely feel interpretation necessary. That they are saving rites, that is, magical performances, he cannot believe—unless he denies reality to all that he knows of life. That they may be colorful and meaningful symbols of what he has achieved and what he hopes to achieve is quite a different matter. When practiced with dignity they can be to him of profound value and aid in making him more acutely aware of his heritage from the past, his union with men and women who in their day, as he is in his, were joined in a crusade to the uplands of life as they knew it.

The future he faces confident and unafraid.

"God's in His heaven—
All's right with the world"

may seem to him a scarcely literal diagnosis of life as he knows it. He may even be very dubious about the comfortable words, "Magna est veritas et praevalebit," and may feel that it will likely be no truer in English than it proved in Latin unless men and women of integrity make it such. The fact that there is so much still to be done: so much ignorance, bigotry, cruelty, blindness to be challenged and jousted with—in a word, "so many loads to lift"—this does not disturb or frighten him. Instead it adds zest to his work, adrenalin to his blood. He may smile at the prophets of doom, present in every age, particularly noisy at the moment, with their cry that now, as never before, America, Christianity, the world, faces a unique and new and "altogether other" crisis—that now for the first time we are standing at the parting of the ways: civilization or chaos; Christianity or communism. He wishes they knew enough of history to make them aware of their absurdity, aware that this world has ever been full of eviction notices, times of crisis, "the flame of a sword which turned every way" effectually barring return to earlier Edens and forcing the tearing of life from a rugged and forbidding—and rich —wilderness. "In times like these what can one man do?" In times like these, he has learned again and again, he can be a man and face the tasks with courage.

Nor does the future beyond the grave terrify or greatly concern him. The fact that through the years men have wondered and surmised, have painted their pictures in terms of their hopes and frustrations—this is known to him and appreciated. So far as the final answer is concerned he is not greatly concerned. He prefers to wait and open his presents on Christmas morning. He is so aware that at every step of the game he is not alone, that he is constantly rubbing shoulders with his fellow contestants, that he himself is far more than the physical body which is his, that the thing which makes him truly himself and not another is that part of him (invisible to the X-ray camera, imponderable on any scales) which is his because he is constantly giving it to others—this is to him so certain that he knows that day by day he is building for himself an immortality that is sure and certain, in the lives of those with whom he labors and loves.

This in itself gives a reality and insistence to the one quality or characteristic of his heritage as a "liberal Protestant": his sense of freedom and its inescapable consequences and responsibilities. He is his own priest, has his own immediate access to the sources of life. He must make his own decisions in the light of what his best endeavor shows him is wise and he must bear the responsibility of his choices, not only in his own life but in the lives of his fellows from whom he cannot, however much he struggles, find escape. This does not destroy the possibility of reverence and worship. Rather it enhances and gives them depth. All life takes on a new and richer quality. He finds himself at each step perpetually in a state of awe before mysteries— mysteries to which he feels himself bidden to penetrate.

No longer does he fear, as did many of his fellows in the past, that if he seeks to see the face of the jealous and capricious Deity he will be smitten dead; that if he eats of the trees of wisdom and of life, he will be thrust out in jealous rage from a beautiful garden and forced to the most awful of all perditions: work. Instead he knows that if he builds his towers toward the sun, he will not be thwarted. Instead, every new unrest and dissatisfaction spurs to new discovery, to new confidence that if he seeks he will truly find; that if he knocks, many doors will be opened to him; and with it all that wholesome knowledge that puts confidence in the head and heart as well as iron into the blood that he must work for what he gets, that there is no possible way to get something for nothing; that he will reap what he sows; that if he sows not, neither will he reap.

> They are here, my richest treasures,
>   Ready for the artist's hand:
> Thou cans't use them; thou cans't mar them;
>   They are flint rock, they are sand.
>
> Be thou careless and unheeding,
>   I will crush thee without rue;
> If thou wilt but learn my lessons—
>   Nothing which thou cans't not do.
>
> I will drive thy ships and engines,
>   Give thee balm for thy distress;
> Will smite thee down unheeding,
>   Will wrap thee in my soft embrace.
>
> Thou must make thine own decisions:
>   If my laws thou hast obeyed,
> Face the future calm and fearless;
>   Thou cans't view me unafraid.

Yes, the liberal Protestant has a *credo,* and it is one that means much to him. It is not rigid in the sense that he will not vary its details as increasing light seems to him to demand. Indeed he is gladly doing that all the time. But his is a credo which he believes is unshakeable. It does not seem to him to be built upon the uncertain sands of historical events which may shift in consequence of tomorrow's flood or the archaeologist's spade. To him it is very dear. He believes that it may prove of interest, perhaps of value, to others like him. He will not attempt to force it upon them. To do that would be to surrender his very title "liberal". He will try to show why he feels as he does; but evidence, not blackjacks, will be his reliance. It will certainly not be a complete blueprint for any of them—it is far from such even for him himself. It may, nonetheless, be of assistance in pointing out to others a few of the many values which one deep-dyed and totally unregenerate liberal has discovered along the highway leading to the far horizon.

SUGGESTIONS FOR FURTHER READING

JULIUS SEELYE BIXLER, *Religion for Free Minds* (New York, 1939).

MORTON S. ENSLIN, "Like a Mighty River", *Crozer Quarterly*, XXVII, 1 (January, 1950).

VERGILIUS FERM, "Oceanic Christianity", *Crozer Quarterly*, XXIII, 1 (January, 1946).

VERGILIUS FERM, *What Can We Believe?* (New York, 1948).

KIRSOPP LAKE, *The Religion of Yesterday and Tomorrow* (Boston, 1925).

CONRAD HENRY MOEHLMAN, *Protestantism's Challenge* (New York, 1939).

FLOYD H. ROSS, *Addressed to Christians* (New York, 1949).

LEROY WATERMAN, *The Religion of Jesus: Christianity's Unclaimed Heritage* (New York, 1952).

RESOURCES AND REALITIES

By

JOHN THOMAS MCNEILL

John Thomas McNeill

One among the treasured books on the shelf of one's library is John T. McNeill's "Makers of Christianity from Alfred the Great to Schleiermacher" (1935). It contains the quintessence of the lives and teachings of some of the commanding figures in Christian history, beautifully written and full of trustworthy scholarship. He is remembered in the profession by his long association with the Divinity School of the University of Chicago where he was professor of the history of European Christianity (1927-1944). Since that time he has been Auburn professor of church history in Union Theological Seminary, New York. A Canadian by birth he has held his ordination relations with the Presbyterian Church. The American Church History Society has long enjoyed his active participation, serving a term as its president. Other of his publications are: "Unitive Protestantism" (1930); "Christian Hope for World Society" (1937); co-authorship of "Medieval Handbooks on Penance" (1938); and the widely approved volume "A History of the Cure of Souls" (1951 and 1952). The Reformation period of history has through the years captured his interest and to it he has given special study. This, besides his own broad interests as an historian of movements, gives this essay on Protestantism a distinction of mature judgment and appraisal worthy of special attention.

Editor

RESOURCES AND REALITIES

JOHN THOMAS MCNEILL

I

IT IS "smart" today to speak contemptuously of Protestantism and Protestants, and most of us have read or heard with patience or alarm the confident forecast that Protestantism is soon to disintegrate or perish of inanity. It is one of the proofs of our vitality that we can absorb without despair a good deal of doleful prognostication and taunting criticism of this sort. No doubt, it is a serious matter that those called Protestants are as such not fraternally beloved by many others called Christians, even though disapproval is modified by "charity" extended from a higher altitude toward the erring. We Protestants must admit too that, viewed as a miscellany of sects, we present a sorry spectacle in the world. I do not know how widely we who contribute to this book, writing in characteristic freedom to say what we will, may differ and seem to contradict each other. Conceivably, this (anticipated) divergence may be taken as fresh and conclusive evidence of the dissolution of what is left of the Reformation. Yet "Protestantism" is something more than a collective noun to embrace the uncounted fragments of church organization that vote against the Papacy. Even its sects do not exist merely in order to be able to "feel superior". For that matter, there exists no branch of Christianity that is not chargeable with sectarianism. Protestantism "protests" and has always protested in terms of affirmation not less than negation. It shares in large measure common loyalties rooted in the past and common hopes for the future. These hopes include that of a united, ecumenical Christianity.

The original principles and inherited resources of Protestantism are not well known within or without the ranks of its adherents. Some suggestion of these will appear in the following paragraphs. It is becoming more evident that the vital differences within the household of Protestantism are less and less denominational. They are differences that arise in the fields of theology and social ethics, and that readily cross denominational frontiers. My own point of approach is that of a liberal evangelical. I decline to capitalize these words lest I should embarrass others who would employ the designation in a more exact and historically identifiable way. I decline too, of course, to interchange substantive and adjective. I do not entertain a liberalism that would reduce Christianity to a shallow mundane ethics professing to obey a Jesus so gentle as to be spineless, and neglecting those minor realities, sin, death, and human tragedy. Nor do I identify myself with "the Evangelicals" whose breath was taken away by the new biblical criticism of the nineteenth century.

St. Paul was, I think, a liberal evangelical. We may call him a Protestant too, not because he rebuked his fallible colleague, Peter, but for the reason that the chief founder of Protestantism thought Paul's thoughts after him more exactly than anyone had ever done. This is true evangelicalism:

> I am not ashamed of the Gospel: it is the power of God
> for salvation to everyone who has faith, to the Jew first
> and also to the Greek. For in it the righteousness of
> God is revealed through faith for faith; as it is written,
> "He who through faith is righteous shall live".
>
> (Rom. 1:16-17).

It was in this free-hearted expression of the experience of the Gospel of faith and power that Luther found entrance into newness of life. Moreover, St. Paul was liberal, with all his evangelical zeal. In his refusal to encourage his converts to call themselves his disciples, in his praise of the charity that rejoices in truth, in his rejection of race barriers in religion, in his use of Stoic ideas and quotation of pagan poets and of a phrase or two from Aristotle, we see the tokens of a mind that firm convictions never closed to life's fresh possibilities.

II

What is this Gospel of which the great Apostle is not ashamed? It is no mere catena of affirmations, like the baptismal formulae and other creeds that later took shape. Christianity was mightily at work while it had no creed but the *Kerygma*, the testimony of its early preachers. It is pointed out by C. H. Dodd that the New Testament word for "preach" (*kerrysein*) is a virtual equivalent of the word "evangelize" (*euaggelisthai*). It belongs to Protestantism to regard the ancient creeds with great reverence but to hold their authority to be derived from the Scripture whose teaching they reaffirm. As forms of words, creeds and confessions are instrumental rather than essential. No blame, to be sure, attaches to those who framed them. It is our fault, rather, that we are reluctant to make our own declarations as our fathers made theirs.

The title of this book suggests that it may function as an essay in that direction. But the word "creed" comes to most minds with an odor of staleness. It raises an impression of something antiquated and confining, a set of tenets clung to through fear of change. A creed may be to a denomination like a regimental flag hung in a cathedral, or a treaty of peace in a library exhibit—the lasting symbol of a prized memory of what can never be again, rather than the current testimony and manifesto it once was. It may be unwholesomely revered as evidence of what is peculiar to an exclusive community of believers, rather than of what is true. Philip Schaff noted that "symbololatry is a species of idolatry".

St. Paul's Gospel antedates the creeds. It also antedates the New Testament books. It is not a distillation of these writings about Christ: it was beginning to give rise to them. It was rather the Word born in a man under the influence of the Spirit of God when he had been confronted and redeemed by Christ. It broke forth from an experience so intense that it could make him say: "Woe to me if I do not preach the Gospel" (I Cor. 9:16). It remade the man himself, controlled and empowered him, and employed his tongue and pen. Paul's "not ashamed" is such an understatement that Moffatt translated it "proud". Yet there were those who, he knew, thought that he ought to be ashamed of it, since it involved a scandalous tale of a teacher who died as a criminal and afterward reigned as a god. The Apostle flings back these reproaches, and exults in his experience of a divine power that can lay hold on men, that can redeem helpless souls when it meets the response of faith. He has found the pure well-spring of spiritual life. One is not ashamed but proud of Good Tidings that he knows to be true.

III

More than any other of the innumerable movements that have stirred the Church, the sixteenth century Reformation recovered this direct and glowing realization of "the power of God to everyone who has faith". It was a great religious revival, and affords the greatest historic exhibit of the immeasurable recuperative possibilities of Christianity. The men who led it were trained in the schools of the Medieval Church. They were ashamed of its accumulated evils, and in the quest of a clear conscience in the midst of a confusion of truth and error, were led through anguish of spirit, and by no previous design of their own, to rediscover the power of faith as St. Paul knew it. These phrases describe Luther's experience: Oecolampedius, Bullinger, Bucer, and Calvin followed with variations the same course. Whether suddenly or slowly, they were inwardly born anew, and filled with gratitude for a redemptive power that had laid hold on them.

The vehemence and vituperation that sometimes found utterance in the Reformers should be judged against the background of the ecclesiastical corruption of their age, and of their situations of anxiety and peril. It is blameworthy, but less so than soft acquiescence in iniquity. It is the waste product of their new religious energy and sense of urgency. An Anglican bishop, Francis Atterbury, in 1687 described Luther as possessing a truly apostolic boldness—"a *parrēsia* such as might have become the days of the apostles". The word is well chosen. It conveys the notion of the outspoken frankness of an emancipated soul, the quality that produces resolute and unreserved free speech. It was exhibited by Peter and John, "uneducated men" who "had been with Jesus", to the wonder of their hearers (Acts 4:7). It is reported, or recommended in a dozen New Testament passages. Similarly vocal and uncompromising were the men of the Reformation. They uttered their assured beliefs before all hearers and in scorn of consequences. They were men who could testify that they had been rescued from the verge of despair, were "born anew" and led through "the open gate of Paradise" (Luther); who were "drawn from the deep mire" and thereafter "burned with a great zeal to go forward" (Calvin).

It does not matter greatly how far Luther's doctrine of justification by faith was anticipated by any of his predecessors. Nor is it important that we should be continually analyzing it into its component parts and summarizing its content. What we often miss in these processes is that the realization of it not only remade the soul of Luther but reshaped for him the whole message of Scripture. Familiar Bible phrases became suddenly dynamic. "Work of God" now meant "that which God works in us"; "power of God" is "that through which he empowers us"; "wisdom of God", "righteousness of God", represent gifts of God to us. Life is enriched and transformed by divine grace and bounty. Ten years after Luther's conversion, in his Preface to the translation of Romans, he explained that faith alone justifies:

> For faith through the merit of Christ obtaineth the Holy Spirit, which Spirit doth make us new hearts, doth exhilarate us, doth excite and inflame our heart, that it may do those things willingly of love which the

law commandeth, and so at the last good works indeed do proceed freely from the faith, which worketh so mightily and which is so lively in our hearts ... yea and doth so embolden the heart of the true believer, that trusting to have God on his side, he is not afraid to oppose himself alone against all creatures.

The translation here quoted is that of "W. W." made in 1594 and republished in 1632: I believe it to be the one heard by John Wesley, May 24, 1738, in an ever memorable Aldersgate Street meeting. The Spirit, says Luther, sets the heart aflame *(cor inflammat)*. Calvin devised a seal depicting a flaming heart offered on an extended hand; Bunyan could say that Luther's *Galatians*, where the same theme is treated, seemed to have been "written out of my heart", and that it made his love for Christ "as hot as fire"; and Wesley's heart was "strangely warmed" while he listened to Luther's stirring words.

The Reformation concept of faith and justification carried with it down the generations joyous celebration of the salvation of Christ, grateful response to the Mercy of God and whole-souled commitment to His Will. It is necessary for theologians to describe it intellectually; but still more useful to realize it in terms of feeling and will:

My heart an altar and Thy love a flame.

Where hearts are not aflame, the power departs from Protestantism—from all Christianity.

IV

But Luther's deliverance unlike Paul's, was closely associated with the reading of the Bible. Wherever he now looked in Scripture, he found illustration and corroboration of the new teaching. The Reformers made the Bible their oracle and their arsenal. They affirmed its authority in strong language. Nobody felt inclined, indeed, to refute their main position.

Thomas Aquinas, with his predecessors, taught that God is the Author of Scripture, even while he affirmed unlimited papal authority over all the faithful. The Reformers enhanced the authority of Scripture by cancelling that of the pope, and by rejecting tradition as a support for unscriptural teaching and practice. No exact equation is possible between the authority of a book and that of a living man. Whatever reverence is paid to Scripture, the living officers of the Church remain, and have their authorized status. Scripture was cited for the monarchical rule of the pope, as well as for the Lutheran and Reformed ministry. Actually, the authority recognized by the late Medieval Church was not strictly that of the Scripture but of the interpretation that the Church had given to it.

Yet the early campaign of Protestantism was victorious largely through its appropriation and direct use of the Bible as the only sufficient revelation of God. Man, born a victim of Adam's sin and deprived of his original righteousness, could by his impaired natural powers attain only to a knowledge of God inadequate for salvation. The true knowledge of God and of salvation is made known only through the Scripture, and to it also we must turn for directives regarding Church order, worship and moral discipline. Lutheranism and typical Anglicanism differ from Reformed Churches on the application of the doctrine of Scripture authority and worship. The latter, would exclude elements of worship not authorized or exemplified in Scripture: the others would admit such as the Scripture does not forbid. Zwingli's negations went even beyond the principle noted, when (competent musician though he was) he abandoned all music in worship. This was really a violent reaction against the frivolous music that had been prevalent. Calvin gave great attention to the cultivation of singing in worship, using the Psalms in vernacular translations; while Luther and his friends laid the foundation of a great development of hymnody. Soon everywhere, evangelical congregations were enjoying the fellowship of sacred song.

"You would not believe", wrote a Walloon student who visited in 1545 the Strasbourg congregation shortly before served by Calvin, "what joy is experienced in singing the praises of the Lord in the mother tongue." The Reformation marched with all ranks singing. Yet Calvin narrowly excluded instrumental music.

In other respects there were differences in early Protestantism's appropriation of the Scripture principle. Lutheranism allowed as matters of indifference (*adiaphora*) some rites that Calvinism rejected as idolatrous. "You extend the class of things indifferent too widely", wrote Calvin to Melanchthon. Even within Lutheranism itself a hot battle was fought over this issue. We all admit, and Protestantism has always admitted, a category of things not to be determined on scriptural authority in the realms of worship and behavior, and even of doctrine. But the area of these *adiaphora* is differently delimited by individuals and churches. If we mention the corporeal presence in the Eucharist, vestments, crucifixes, bowing at the name of Jesus, episcopacy, dancing, gambling, and obedience to a tyrant, we recall a few of the varied matters that some reject as neither authorized nor "indifferent", others find admissible or even required.

There is no ready reckoner for things indifferent, and we do well not only to tolerate what we ourselves regard as such, but to accord to others the right to form their own categories of the *adiaphora* in accordance with their own consciences. We are fully persuaded of the principle enunciated by Roger Williams just three centuries ago (1652): "I desire not that liberty to myself which I would not freely and impartially weigh out to all consciences of the world beside". Protestantism has not always taken this ground, and not all Protestants take it today. Yet on the whole we have abandoned the spirit and the practice of persecution,—in which we always were, relatively, half-hearted,—and have confined our intolerance to words. In the case of some forms of evil, to tolerate is to foster. Inevitably we form our codes and casuistries, but these are subject to revision. We shall always be obliged to make fresh decisions on the limits of our toleration.

V

For Calvinists the Bible became the norm of Church polity and discipline, as well as of doctrine and worship. Finding in the New Testament no evidence of an order of bishops as distinct from preaching presbyters, and working in a center from which the bishop had previously been expelled in disgrace, Calvin reorganized the Church without the episcopate. He did not disapprove of bishops as they were in the age of the Church Fathers, or where, as in England, they rejected the Papacy and favored reform. But he repudiated the notion that an order of bishops is necessary to the existence of a true church. The Scottish Reformed Church cast off the episcopate when this was thrust upon it by secular authority, and voiced indiscriminate condemnation of "prelacy". This position would probably not have been taken had the controversy not been intensified by a form of worship similarly imposed by the King. There exists in Presbyterianism no well-grounded objection in principle to a responsible and constitutional episcopate that would be adapted to a conciliar or representative system of church government. That bishops are the sole successors of the Apostles and bear a peculiar divine commission —a position quite without convincing historical support—remains an unacceptable theory to Protestants in general, even while they do not desire to exclude those who hold it from their spiritual company.

To found any modern system of polity upon the New Testament is rendered increasingly difficult. The evidence seems to indicate wide variety and fluctuation, and development by adjustment to conditions. It is probably safe to assume that neither "presbyter" nor "bishop" was a term technically conceived in the early decades of the Church. It is clear that the Church and the ministry were regarded as of divine institution, but it is also evident that no precise pattern of the form of either was held to be of any such authority or permanence.

Protestantism in each generation accepts the changes imposed by fresh understanding of the Bible and of the Church's task. We ought frankly to recognize weaknesses in the Protestant position that are associated with its stress upon the authority of the Bible. It was affirmed by Zwingli, and formally stated in the Ten Conclusions of Bern in 1528, that "the Church was born of the Word of God" *(nata est ex Dei verbo)*. Luther in a work of 1539 cites a similar phrase as from Augustine, "the Church is begotten *(generatur)* nourished and strengthened by the Word of God" *(On the Councils and Churches,* Part III). This is close to the Barthian emphasis; the Church is dependent upon the Scripture, and judged by it. The historical view of the Bible leads rather to the position that the Old Testament came from the matrix of devout Judaism and the New Testament from the experience of the primitive Church.

It is necessary to be utterly frank in our recognition of the known historical facts. A faith that is professed in defiance of facts that are known is simply not sincerely professed. We dare not, as Calvin warns, reject truth wherever it may appear, if we would not affront the Spirit of God, the one source of truth *(Institutes* II, ii, 15). It is true in a large sense that "the Bible was begotten in the womb of the Church" (Allen Richardson). We do not know the full story of New Testament origins: recent research seems to leave us in increasing uncertainty. But we cannot doubt that the Gospels and Epistles took shape in response to emerging conditions in the Church where men were moved to instruct it and guide its course by their testimony. All other results of biblical criticism are secondary to this in their challenge to Protestantism. So long as "Word of God" is identified with "Holy Scripture", and confined to the written page, the statement that the Church was born of it calls for correction.

It is appropriate to ask in what degree the Reformers identify Word and Scripture. Luther valued very differently the various books of the Bible in accordance with their commen-

dation and illumination of faith and redemption of Christ. He
thought James "an epistle of straw" for its emphasis on works
to the neglect of faith, and the Apocalypse "not the work of
an apostle or a prophet". Calvin, according to his eminent
contemporary, Jean Bodin, when asked why he had not written
a commentary on this book candidly admitted that he was
"totally at a loss regarding its meaning". Luther in his Galatians commentary appeals against adversaries who cite a thousand scripture passages on good works, "to the Lord himself who is above the Scriptures". There exists for him too,
an authority of "the external Word, orally preached by men
like you and me . . . For God's Word cannot be present without God's people, and God's people without God's Word".
It is thus not purely a matter of spelled out words within a
holy book.

The Scripture, too, is for the Reformers the instrument as
well as the utterance of the Holy Spirit. The "inner witness
of the Spirit" is necessary to the comprehension of its message.
"No man", declared Zwingli, "can understand God's Word
unless he is illuminated by God". And the human authors of
it were not merely recording instruments; they spake as they
were moved by the Spirit. The Magnificat, Luther pointed out,
flowed from Mary's personal experience of, and illumination
by, the Holy Spirit. Thus the Bible is vitally and spiritually
related to both its writers and its readers in such a way that
its message is determined by the action of the living Spirit of
God.

To the Reformers, the Word is in the Scripture, as Henri
Clavier says of Calvin "not statistically but dynamically". In
Paul T. Fuhrmann's language, inspiration is for Calvin not
"mechanical" but "organic". Calvin stresses the excellence of
Scripture above other writings on the ground that in it, as not
elsewhere, "we perceive the majesty of God" *(Institutes* I,
vii, 4). In Heinrich Heppe's judgment, God is for Calvin the
Author not so much of the text of Scripture as of the doctrine
attested in it. He certainly taught the progressive character

of revelation: it was accommodated at each step to the growing capacity of men to receive truth. Adam saw the first "feeble sparks" of that splendor which in Christ has illumined the world; and the Old Testament conveys only "types" and foreshadowings of that glorious redemption that becomes manifest in the New.

But there remains a sense in which the Church has been born in the written Word. From Acts to Irenaeus, no less than in later writings, we see clearly that the Christians clung to the Old Testament as an indispensable source of their message. Further, the New Testament books were instrumental in the making of the Church, through the conversion of those without no less than the edification of those within. The Scriptures have had a church-forming function, and ever since the New Testament books were separately written they have furnished the primary stuff of the Gospel message wherever it has been preached.

Considerations of this sort link the early Protestant, largely uncritical, conception of the authority of Scripture with that which is possible for us today. The Reformers were most anxious to set the Bible free from the limitations imposed by a tradition alleged to be original, and from the ecclesiastically motivated interpretations placed upon it, as well as from the close, restriction of its circulation practiced by the hierarchy. Some of their followers heightened and narrowed their views of the inspiration of Scripture, so as to set new crippling limitations upon the operation of God's Spirit. The words of Bishop Nicholas F. S. Gruntvig, the reviver of the Danish Church a century ago, are appropriate here, and still need to be stressed:

> The Christian communion is no mere reading club. It is a fellowship of faith begotten and preserved through the spoken word as this goes down from generation to generation.

It is not by leaving the Bible behind that we may experience a revival and increment of the spiritual life within and among us. If we read the Bible with studious attention and spiritual expectation, and with an awareness of our own world and its needs, it becomes a life-giving and communion-forming agent, and the Christian fellowship is begotten anew.

VI

If there is one Reformation doctrine that has been more misunderstood than others, it is the doctrine of "the priesthood of all believers". This doctrine was frequently enunciated by Luther, and is vital to Protestant practical churchmanship. It has commonly been associated with an individualistic concept of "private judgment", in accordance with which every man proclaims himself his own priest and his own theologian. It is true that Luther wished to open the direct way from the soul to God. But he never imagined that we are individually so separated or so competent as this. His teaching on the priesthood is rather that in his calling "every man may be useful or beneficial to the rest". By this priesthood also "we are able to appear before God, to pray for others, and to teach one another mutually the things that are of God". "A Christian does not live in himself, but in Christ and his neighbor". The gifts of God "flow from one to the other". Thus the priesthood of believers is rather to be associated with the corporate life of Christians, the communion of saints in the visible Church, than with any self-assertive and clamorous rejection of official priesthood. Priesthood as prayer for others, and cure of souls, is extended by Luther from the clergy to the whole body. The meaning is not so much "every man his own priest", as "every man his neighbor's priest, intercessor, and counsellor".

Martin Bucer applied this principle in numerous writings, and in the group organization of the Strasbourg church. Mutual exhortation and consolation by laymen and ministers formed an essential feature of the church life of Geneva. Calvin not only secured stated meetings of the ministers for this purpose, but ultimately also of the magistrates. Attendance at these sessions for mutual criticism was obligatory, and, the councillors were required, under solemn pledge of secrecy, and in an atmosphere of religion, to deal frankly with each other. Spener and the Pietists, the Moravian Church reconstituted under Zinzendorf, as well as John Wesley and "the people called Methodists" in their several ways made careful provision for the exercise of this mutual and fraternal discipline by which Christians in training, whatever their rank or vocation, made themselves spiritually and morally available to each other.

We need to make it understood that this priesthood of mutual help is good historic Protestantism, and to attempt, and expect, its practice. Ours is not properly a unilateral discipline, nor an exclusive teaching privilege, exercised by the clergy. The growing complexity of the social pattern and of the skills and specialties involved in it, makes more necessary, and potentially fruitful, the mutual contribution of each to all. We tend to pursue selfish courses and to prize private gain; but there is in the Gospel a power to reverse this inclination, to turn our interests toward what we may give rather than what we may get, and to make the blessings we share the measure of our happiness.

Very naturally the priesthood of each Christian in behalf of his neighbor works itself out in political, economic and cultural relationships. All the Reformers were very far from resting economic behavior upon self-interest: our calling is our service, and our gains in it are administered in stewardship. Whatever later Calvinists taught, or admitted, in this area, Calvin himself denounced in countless vigorous or even blistering statements the notion that prosperity in this world is the evidence, or the fruit, of godliness. This is a view, he says, that "proceeds from the devilish error that men's souls are mortal" (On Job 21:7). The blessings of the righteous are associated with the life to come and with our present meditation thereon. We daily see the impious gain vast wealth; but our felicity consists in the heavenly enjoyment of the presence of God, of which we now have a foretaste only *(Institutes* III, vii, 8: ix, 3-4).

Protestantism has characteristically asserted the right to hold private property, but not to use it with a lawless freedom. It blesses such business enterprise only as is undertaken with a view to the benefit of all whom it affects. Richard Baxter, commenting on economic duty, wrote simply: "The public good is the Christian's life". Profits, interest, rents, taxes, philanthropies, all come rigorously under this law. Wesley's teaching in this realm is that if by diligence we gain and by frugality we save, it is that we may give so as to bless our neighbor. The good Protestant is "stingy" where expenditures for pleasures are concerned, but liberal toward "good causes". Not all Protestants are exemplary here, to be sure,—far from it. But it is not uncommon to see one who has been too intent upon gain, attaining maturity, or smitten by conscience, turn about and become intent upon the art of helpful giving.

VII

Protestantism has been greatly indebted to its thoughtful critics. But there is a type of supercilious sophisticate who would dismiss it by contemptuous generalizations. One of these judgments takes the form: "Protestantism has no saints". It presupposes, or betrays, an abysmal ignorance of religious biography. It is true that we take our saints for granted: they are not canonized or adored, nor (to our shame) even well remembered. But they are a countless number, most of them in humble station, living dedicated lives in their families and vocations. Henri Hauser has well described the fruit of the Reformation in the words, "the laicization of saintliness". Our saints do not seek merit by bodily austerities; but their "practice of the presence of God", their fervor in prayer and self-renunciation in service are not surpassed in any non-Protestant communion, or in any religion.

[113]

Another way in which one may reassure himself and his circle of his superiority to Protestants is to imply that they are "Philistines"—persons of no cultural refinement or sensibility. When this word was much in vogue in England, James Anthony Froude reported that an Oxford professor called Luther a Philistine, an enemy of culture—"such", he adds, "as the professor himself". Froude's thrust may have been unfair: but nothing is more common than to claim a reputation for a cultivated mind by the simple device of charging another with boorishness. The history of schools of higher learning, of literature and art, and the relative status with respect to education and intelligence of Protestant and other areas of the world, lend no support to this unfavorable judgment. Luther was widely familiar with the classics, a gifted musician, a lover of nature's beauty. Calvin has numerous passages of rare eloquence in appreciation of the beauty of God's handiwork in the stars, in field and stream, and in the human form. Countless Protestant writers, including some theologians, have surpassed him in this regard. Jonathan Edwards in the solitary contemplation of nature more than once experienced mystical illumination and profound emotion:

> Once as I rode out into the woods for my health, in 1737, having alighted from my horse in a retired place, as my manner commonly has been, to walk, for divine contemplation and prayer, I had a view that for me was extraordinary of the glory of the Son of God . . . which continued as near as I can judge about an hour, which kept me . . . in a flood of tears.

And John Wesley sometimes found time to remark on the fair landscapes, of which he saw many, in such phrases as:

> the gently declining sun, the stillness of the evening, the beauty of the meadows, and fields through which "the smooth clear river drew his sinuous train" . . . (*Journal*, July 5, 1770)

Or he may note on his journeys "a lovely country . . . the road delightfully pleasant . . . beside a clear river" (April 23, 1784). As poet and musical genius, respectively, John Milton and John Sebastian Bach are not easily matched outside of Protestantism. It has been conclusively shown by Percy Scholes that the old-time Puritans were rather more than their contemporaries interested in music and song.

Yet we do well to take to heart the charge of Philistinism, as a warning to avoid a deplorable possibility. It may be that we are losing ground in the education that secures appropriation of the intellectual and aesthetic heritage of mankind. This generation is captivated by the whirr of wheels, ingenious in the invention of gadgets, and in general concerned only in the most superficial way with beauty in nature, art, or literature. The *sapiens et eloquens pietas* sought by John Sturm in the Strasbourg academy, and by Calvin and Beza in Geneva,— an ideal long cultivated in Protestant schools, as the foundation documents of Harvard (1636) and of Union Theological Seminary (1836) attest,—has today little appeal to the majority. Solid learning and sound culture come only by slow processes that are alien to this age of jet propulsion, and are all too rarely prized as they deserve by university students, from among whom ministers are recruited. It is not possible either to slow the engines or greatly to quicken the cultural processes. Perhaps it is possible, however, to restore a just estimate of values, and to revive the disciplines that emancipate and enrich the mind. We must not fail to live in the contemporary world; but we are lost if we cannot escape imprisonment within it, or if we fail to expound the Christian message from an intellectual perspective that takes in its sweep the culture of mankind. The Protestant is free to gain this perspective, if he has patience, energy and courage.

VIII

Since the beginning of the Reformation, Roman Catholicism has been our disturbing companion. It has condemned, persecuted, criticized, derided and imitated us, and vastly stimulated our activities. We have returned these attentions in kind, although in unequal measure. It was hostile criticism by the Reformers, more than anything else, that brought about the Counter-Reformation; and where Roman Catholicism is not challenged by Protestantism it displays peculiarly the need of reform. Correspondingly, where one variety of Protestantism is dominant, deterioration almost invariably sets in. The wide differences between Protestantism and Roman Catholicism seem to offer insuperable obstacles to any reunion of them. One of the principal differences lies simply in the attitude to reform. The Reformation was not completed in the sixteenth century: it is never completed. We may for the sake of comfort try to transform Protestantism into a closed system; but it breaks out again. It has no "infallible" voice to silence other voices in decrees that are "irreformable". Protestantism cannot be static. In its state churches and strong denominations it may try to be so, but the result is often commotion and schism. Whereas Roman Catholicism has sent off disaffected fragments of some importance, and sometimes antagonized majorities of the populations in lands where it had privileged status, Protestantism has subdivided into sects so numerous as to bewilder the observer. Most of the sects represent the impatient spirit of reform that could not wait for the majority.

Bishop Bossuet supposed that the "variations of Protestantism" would destroy it, and his point of view has been frequently reaffirmed, while Protestantism grows. The varieties for the most part hold in common a great body of Protestant tenets, including that of an unqualified repudiation of the papal monarchy. It is sometimes forgotten that most of them also hold in outline the orthodox Protestant doctrine of the One, Holy, Catholic Church, the perpetually cherished Spouse of Christ, that endures through all time and is spread abroad through all the earth. This doctrine has always been affirmed in Protestantism, and has been elaborated upon by its chief theologians. It has come to a new vitality today, and a revival of Protestant ecumenicity is in full course. But in this movement Protestant churches are associated with others with whose points of view Protestants have not been familiar. Mutual discoveries are being made between us and the Eastern Orthodox, Old Catholics and Anglo-Catholics; and if agreements are not reached, at least antagonisms are largely overcome.

Some Protestants, who think themselves more scriptural than the rest of us, denounce the liberalism that makes possible these contacts, and seek to establish a "fundamentalist" world communion. It is perfectly evident that the note of world-wideness, always characteristic of active Christianity, is dominant today. Many of the more eccentric sects are themselves striving to span the world with their mission posts. Most Christians no longer need to be persuaded that their Church is more than local, or national in scope. A number of the leading Protestant churches are increasingly ready to live in brotherly love with each other, and to share their theological insights and practical experiences. But between these and the group of churches that stand fast for tradition, the degree of mutual persuasion and approach is not yet greatly different from what it has been. Those who, for example, have traditionally regarded as normal or necessary certain symbolic elaborations of public worship, or belief in the "corporeal presence", continue to hold these positions, and those who have found these to be distracting intrusions rather than aids to spiritual worship or faith, have not changed their views. Whenever we press for agreement in such matters, we are invariably brought to a halt. We are simply not persuading one another. We are learning, however, to speak more fraternally of one another, and in some measure to avoid the old habitual misstatements by each of the other's position.

It is a defensible statement that a liberal evangelical Protestantism is more truly catholic than the rest of Christianity. The Reformers charged the papacy with sectarianism, since it condemned Greeks and Bohemians on the ground that they withheld obedience from Rome. We do not wish to exclude from communion those whose Master is Christ, whatever their peculiarities; and we desire a reciprocation of this attitude. Some will say that this is a dangerous laxity: but is there not greater danger in an insistence on restrictions that have no sanction in Apostolic Christianity? "Is Christ divided? Was Paul crucified for you?"

Not only in the West, but everywhere in the world, Protestantism is now confronted by its natural rival, Roman Catholicism. All the facts indicate that the controversy will continue. Its future stages cannot be predicted. The Roman Church flourishes where it is a minority in a relaxed and half-secularized Protestant community. In the English-speaking nations it is increasingly visible and aggressive. Many Protestants fail to realize that it is not the kind of church in morale and morality that Erasmus satirized and the Reformers denounced. It moves ahead of us in intellectual power, in effective propaganda and appeal to the people. It exhibits an institutional devotion that is capable of martyrdom. It has been turning to the use of the Bible, and its spokesmen employ the language of the Reformers in appealing to "the Word of God". Yet it will have no fraternity with us, but views us as deluded schismatics and heretics who must repent and obey. Its hierarchical leaders seem intent upon a power that is not of the Spirit, and does not promise liberty. These ends, insofar as they are a menace to liberty, must be frustrated. The only effective check will come from a Protestantism that is spiritually and intellectually revived, a new generation of believers "not ashamed of the Gospel" and equipped to expound it in all its implications for human life.

One of the realities that we must recognize, then, is that Roman Catholicism is our determined rival. While it embraces many friendly and charitable Christians, officially it comes with assured assertion of absolute claims that are utterly unacceptable to us. It makes no secret of the desirability of the extinction of Protestantism. If we are farsighted we shall not pray, as our predecessors sometimes did, for the complete overthrow of the papacy. I take this position not on the ground that it is a bulwark against leftist totalitarianism: it seems, indeed, to offer as much incitement as resistance to communism. But I believe we need it as a wholesome stimulation to our morale. We are not, let us confess, so spiritually vigorous as to be able safely to do without the challenge of its adverse criticism and activity. Even the fact that Protestantism is given a gloomy prognosis helps to keep us alert and forward-looking. The triumph of Rome would be a calamity; but its downfall in the near future would mean to us the loss of a helpful adversary. It would mean also the loss of not a little positive helpfulness in realms of learning and piety. We are bound to reject both Rome's monarchical claims and her superstitious cults. But we need to set ourselves to a fuller understanding of these, and of other elements of the Roman system. A well-grounded historical and philosophical knowledge of that system is of first-rate importance for ministers and laymen, both of the older and of the younger churches. Its complexity is such that it cannot be grasped in short and easy lessons: and it is sure to be misunderstood by those who observe only outward and contemporary facts.

IX

It is possible, however, through absorption in fear of an improbable mastery of the world by the papacy, to allow ourselves to be overtaken by a greater and more imminent calamity. The spirit of irreligion is much more prevalent than devotion to the papal monarchy: and this spirit is not our rival but our enemy. It has its fullest expression in communist areas of the world, but it is a menace everywhere. It sifts religious elements out of education, and inculcates in the schools the assumption that religion is a vestigial survival, at most a matter of curious intellectual interest, beneath the practical concern of educated people. Life has indeed no concerns that reach beyond the present social order, no need to seek a moral law beyond social custom. The acceptance of this view, however, destroys the validity and permanence of social custom itself. Society gradually drops its habits. The moral standards that go with the Christian religion are reduced to the status of folkways of no abiding authority. Earnest youth is left bewildered and adrift, while crimes of violence and political corruption disgrace our communities. It is not easy, as we look about us, to feel assured of the continuity of free societies. Where the convictions on which these societies have rested crumble, the structures are endangered. Communists are ready to impose authority; but, in terms of the needs of the human spirit, their prescription is worse than anarchy itself.

The intellectual strength of anti-religion, whether totalitarian or simply irresponsible, is not very great, although it claims superior enlightenment and obtains the support of some philosophies. Protestantism is intellectually, not less than ecclesiastically, unco-ordinated. It has little real weight in higher education, despite a show of names on university boards. Its theological schools have little to do with one another, and within the same faculties there may be not only wide diversities, but little vital intellectual intercourse. I do not suggest that we should press for unity of thought; but we might well provide better than we do for the sharing of ideas. To be abreast of the demands and opportunities that confront us, we need to parallel the World Council of Churches with a master school, employing the ablest teachers of theology and the higher culture to be found, attended by students from all nations, serving to acquaint each with the traditions and principles of all, and with the spiritual experience of mankind. Protestantism will not reach ecumenicity in the full sense until something of this sort has been undertaken. We need, moreover, to employ the inventions of science in the service of religion, in the training of ministers and the teaching of youth, instead of surrendering these new devices to secular uses. We are experimenting with "audio-visual aids", but we have no general Protestant guidance regarding what it is that is to be *aided*. There is a hap-hazard growth of the use of radio and television by preachers and evangelists, but how slight and ephemeral, if not objectionable, is much of the material presented! It does not, I fear, give much evidence that Protestants have anything to teach, or that they can render a reason for the faith that is in them.

The ecumenical revival of Protestantism has been largely an outgrowth of missionary expansion and the consequent enlargement of the Church's interests and outlook. The mission of Christianity in the past century and a half has had multiple and immeasurable effects upon the world. In Asia, Africa and the South Pacific Islands, old faiths and patterns of social life have been challenged. In some instances a new national consciousness has been stirred up as a secondary and unplanned result of the disturbing leaven of Christianity. Protestant churches have arisen, and their members have met and are meeting, like the early Christians with varying degrees of steadfastness, the perils of a hostile environment. The old religions have themselves felt a profound influence from the altruistic spirit and social concern shown by the Christian groups; they have also become imitative of Christianity in missionary enterprise and methods of propaganda. A Buddhist organization in New York City holds preaching services, and is popularly called a "church". Although with the increase of migration we may expect some penetration of western countries by the religions of Asia, their power to expand widely at the expense of Christianity is not apparent. Religious expansion is very largely a Christian phenomenon. In this process Protestantism is able, through comity arrangements and national organizations, to act increasingly as a unit. It is beginning to "take the world for its parish". This is hardly more than St. Paul did. The words quoted above from Romans 1 are preceded by the declaration: "I am eager to preach the gospel to you also who are in Rome". Rome was the world's capital, the world in miniature. Jews, Greeks and barbarians are held before the Apostle's eye in this chapter; just as in the other old world center, Athens, the message is to "all men everywhere". (Acts 17:30) We have begun to recover the bold enterprise of the original gospel missionaries.

The association in the World Council and affiliated agencies of the "Younger Churches" with those of the West has begun to show a remarkable measure of unity on moral issues and even in the realm of social and political principles. The centrifugal forces of Protestantism appear largely to have spent themselves, and the trend is definitely toward fuller understanding, cooperation and communion. Whereas in former centuries the union of the churches was ardently advocated by a few, there was lacking the awareness of the world that we possess, and the fraternal intercourse of churches in all continents was not thinkable. Today, not only a few ministers and scholars are proposing Christian union: the ecumenical spirit is reaching the lay membership of the churches in an encouraging degree.

X

It is not in the statistics, activities and attitudes of the churches that our times are seen in their darkest aspect. But undoubtedly a spiritual darkness prevails outside the churches, and to the degree that they are enfeebled by secularism, penetrates them. Future generations will remember that in this mid-century man moved in an atmosphere of gloom. Experience has made us wary of hope. Many of us are like the shocked and orphaned Korean tots who even under kind treatment long remain unable to smile. Indeed, to admit that there is anything to smile over, becomes a kind of heresy. The gloom has been spread by poets, theologians and educational pundits, reacting against the assumptions of their predecessors of a less unhappy generation. Every visiting orator now begins his discourse with the reminder that we live in an era of disillusionment and insecurity. The Gospel was good news: but this is neither good nor news.

When I was very young I learned that man's chief end is to glorify God and enjoy Him forever. If this should be true, all the bad news that is merely mundane may not invalidate the Good News. It is true that human life today is tragic with distress and anguish. Our depression is due not so much to the deterioration of conditions as to the disappointment of rosy hopes. We were trying to find enjoyment not in God but in the fruits of science. Man is approaching mastery of the forces of nature, only to have his heart stabbed with fear of destruction. He has employed his endowment of reason and imagination, his skill of hand and eye, with results that are marvellous. His efforts bring the possibility of longer life and greater comfort than his fathers knew—yet modern man has not mentally resolved the major problems that troubled the ancients—the meaning of the world and of life, and how to order societies in peace. With all our machines, men and women and children in great numbers starve and shudder with cold, and the victims of wrong still utter their ceaseless cry. Fear and anxiety haunt the recesses of consciousness, with effects disastrous to personality and community.

Will the latter part of this century see progress toward deliverance from the evils that dog human existence? I am not one of those who despair of progress. But nothing is more illusory than progress in scientific skills and material power without the realization that man's true orientation is Godward. If man has dominion over the creatures it is not that he should become merely a king of beasts. Power without true piety brings only corruption and oppression; but where the Spirit of the Lord is, there is liberty. The gateway to a golden future for man is not closed. But we shall reach it only if we reach beyond it. The only true basis for a sound criticism of bad politics is found in a realm beyond politics; the only philanthropy or social endeavor that will permanently serve society's victims is a response to the love of God that turns toward His suffering children. Life is whole, and earth must cling to heaven or perish. The failure of merely secular courses of action calls us back to faith. Here we find the real "challenge and response" of this hour. We may not "return to the Reformation;" rather we must return to that to which the Reformation returned, "the power of God for salvation to everyone that has faith". I wrote above, "The Gospel was good news". Let the tense be corrected: it *is* good news, and there is no other tidings so momentous that we can hear or speak.

SUGGESTIONS FOR FURTHER READING

W. K. ANDERSON (editor), *Protestantism: a Symposium* (Nashville, 1944).

JOHN CALVIN, *Institutes of the Christian Religion,* translated by John Allen, two volumes (Philadelphia, 1936).

C. H. DODD, *Apostolic Preaching and Its Developments* (Chicago, 1937).

R. N. FLEW and R. E. DAVIES (editors), *The Catholicity of Protestantism* (London, 1950).

P. T. FUHRMANN, "Calvin, the Expositor of Scripture", *Interpretation,* VI (1952), 188-209.

W. E. GARRISON, *A Protestant Manifesto* (New York, 1952).

H. HAUSER, *La naissance du Protestantisme* (Paris, 1940).

H. HEPPE, *Reformed Dogmatics* (translated by G. T. Thomson), (London, 1950).

MARTIN LUTHER, *Works of Martin Luther,* with introductions and notes, six volumes (Philadelphia, 1930-43).

J. T. MCNEILL, *Books of Faith and Power* (New York, 1947).

J. H. NICHOLS, *A Primer of Protestantism* (New York, 1947).

W. PAUCK, *The Heritage of the Reformation* (Boston, 1950).

A. RICHARDSON and W. SCHWEITZER (editors), *Biblical Authority for Today* (London, 1951).

W. L. SPERRY (editor), *Religion and Our Divided Denominations* (Cambridge, Mass., 1945).

N. SYKES, *The Crisis of the Reformation* (London, 1948).

A PROTESTANT CONCEPTION OF RELIGIOUS AUTHORITY

By
JOHN COLEMAN BENNETT

John Coleman Bennett

When one thinks of the name of John Bennett one thinks of social Christianity, for it is in this area of Christian thought that he has made some significant contributions. His book titles support this association: "Social Salvation" (1935); "Christianity and Our World" (1936); "Christian Realism" (1941); "Christian Ethics and Social Policy" (1946); and particularly that fine little book so well received by the public "Christianity and Communism" (1948). To a number of symposia he has contributed essays—all characteristic of his thought—notably to the volumes "The Church Faces the World" (1939) and "Liberal Theology" (1942). Born a Canadian he has been educated in American colleges, taking his master's degree at Mansfield College at Oxford. His divinity alma mater, Union Theological Seminary of New York, now claims him a staff member as professor of Christian theology and ethics (since 1943). He has also taught at Auburn Theological Seminary and at the Pacific School of Religion and has served as special lecturer at a number of American universities and colleges. He has been honored by the Church Divinity School of the Pacific and the Pacific School of Religion with the doctor of divinity degree. For many years he has participated actively in the ecumenical movement serving on the committee of the church and the economic order and on the committee of Social Action of his church (Congregational). His ethical and practical interests have not clouded his theological bent of mind so that his judgment upon the essential genius of Protestantism is not only that of practical concern for the larger issues involved but for the fundamental questions of ideology which undergird any mature discussion of the subject.

Editor

A PROTESTANT CONCEPTION OF RELIGIOUS AUTHORITY

JOHN COLEMAN BENNETT

WHERE do we find the chief source of authority for faith and doctrine and moral decision? There is no more fundamental question for Protestants to ask and there is no question to which it is more difficult to give a fully satisfactory answer.

This problem of authority is especially urgent and difficult for Protestants whose minds have been formed in part by liberal criticism of orthodoxies, because they have rejected all external authorities that are to be accepted without question. They have no closed system of thought which they regard it as a duty to defend against all critics. Much is said in these days about the status of liberalism but one thing is quite clear: liberalism as the endless criticism of all external authorities, of all infallibilities, of all closed theological systems is very much alive. I believe that we must always be grateful for it as a precious heritage.

Two or three decades ago when Christians still felt the glow of deliverance from a hard traditionalism of the Fundamentalist type, and when modern man was still quite sure of himself, the problem of religious authority was obscured. In those days the liberal Protestant was deeply influenced by the authority of whatever an enlightened modern man thought that he could believe. There was an appeal, whether recognized or not, to the up-to-date, to the assumptions that went with the science of the period, to deeply held convictions concerning man and his future which dominated the culture. There were all shades of this faith of modernity. Often it was completely secular. Often it was restrained and corrected by strong Christian influences. There is a danger of caricaturing individual thinkers of an earlier period by attributing to them certain general tendencies that we discern as characteristic of their period without allowing for the fact that many of them were dependent upon the Bible and the Church tradition as well as upon the thought of the period. Also they were held back from some of the more fantastic illusions of the time by a measure of common sense. Still it remains true that liberal Christians of a generation ago did find it relatively easy to decide what elements of the Bible and of the Christian tradition to accept or reject because they were guided by the self-confident modern mind.

Today that self-confident modern mind has gone. The shock that came from the discovery that a whole generation of wise men in the Church and outside the Church could be gravely mistaken has made many of us sceptical not only about the traditional religious authorities but also about all philosophies and all systems of reason. It is now much clearer than it was before the break in modern man's confidence that the unrecognized pressure of a culture upon man's use of his reason may be the most tyrannical of all authorities.

In this chapter I shall have to pass over the steps by which the Christian mind comes to the decision that the ultimate authority is to be found in the Christian revelation. One may be driven in the first instance by the breakdown of the modern faiths that have so often—even in the Church—taken the primary place in the minds of men. This is insufficient in itself but it is important preparation. I suspect that this negative preparation never stands alone. A real anticipation of a positive faith in Christ goes with it. This may have its source in the earliest Christian influences that have touched us. While one is pushed by the failure of every other faith one is drawn by the grace and truth that are in Christ. And then one may find that quite unexpected answers to old questions begin to appear as one lives longer with Christian truth. Some such pilgrimage as this is at least familiar to many contemporary Protestants. Now the question is: Where is the ultimate authority to a person who is in the midst of this pilgrimage?

The essential Protestant answer to this question concerning the location of religious authority is easy to state in general terms. The idea that the essence of Protestantism is religious individualism is a strange modern misconception. The Protestant authority is the revelation of God in Christ known to us through the Bible. We can begin to understand what that sentence means if we raise three questions about it. 1) What is the relation between this revelation of God and the Bible as a whole? 2) What is the relation between the Biblical revelation and the Church? 3) What is the relation between what is given through both Bible and Church and the insight, the conscience, the faithful response of the individual Christian?

1. Take the first question about the relation between the revelation and the Bible as a whole. Every person and every Christian group does appeal to the Bible selectively. Even the advocate of the most extreme doctrine of plenary inspiration emphasizes some parts of the Bible more than others. Martin Luther set a bold example of selecting those books of the Bible which were for him the bearers of revelation and of rejecting other books.

The first effect of modern historical criticism of the Bible was to encourage drastic elimination of large parts of the Bible that were regarded as poor history or outmoded science or as belonging to the primitive stages of religious development. The general tendency was to select parts of the Bible as having religious authority on the basis of emphases which came from the contemporary culture. This led to a tendency to underestimate the Old Testament as a whole, though the prophets were highly valued as the first exponents of the Social Gospel. It caused many Christians to put almost exclusive emphasis on the Synoptic Gospels, to eliminate from them all traces of eschatology, and to see in Paul the chief perverter of Christianity.

In recent years there has appeared a quite different approach to the Bible among Protestant Biblical scholars and theologians who fully accept the methods and results of Biblical criticism. I believe that this approach has great promise. It begins by taking seriously the faith of the Biblical writers themselves that they are telling about a long succession of divine acts of revelation and redemption. Starting with that assumption one is impressed less by the variety than by the unity in the Bible. The variety is there and it is extremely important to avoid the tendency that is now a serious temptation to force a unified pattern on the whole Bible, a temptation which is the opposite of that which was most commonly felt a generation ago.

I shall speak of two ways in which we can see the unity in the Bible.

In the first place, there is a recognizably Biblical way of thinking about God and man and history. This can be seen when the Bible is contrasted with mystical and speculative religious philosophies. Nearly everyone who writes about theology in these days dwells at length on the uniqueness of the Biblical conception of history. Biblical ways of thinking about ultimate questions have been regarded as crude and untidy by the wise men of most periods but today many wise men are sufficiently discouraged about their own wisdom so that they look upon the Bible with expectation.

More significant is the discovery that the Bible has a center of its own. In relation to this center most of the Bible can be seen to have meaning for us. This is different from saying that the Bible has a high point or a few high points and that the rest of it can be allowed to fall into the background. The New Testament as a whole is about God's act in Christ. To understand what this means for the Christian we need the epistles as much as the gospels. In fact the idea of a conflict between the Epistles and the Gospels is now regarded as untenable by most scholars. God's act in Christ can only be understood as the fulfillment of a series of acts of God about which we read in the Old Testament. The Old Testament is a record of a preparatory revelation which is incomplete without the fulfillment in the New Testament. But this preparatory revelation has its own value and needs to be studied on its own terms. Much of what Christians know about God they learn from the Old Testament. This is especially true of the working of God in the events of history. The New Testament is normative but it is not an independent norm that can be understood by itself. I am not thinking only of the fact that without the Old Testament the student would be unable to understand the origin or the meaning of New Testament ideas and images. That is obvious enough and it is involved in what I shall now say. It is less obvious but extremely important that without the Old Testament the New Testament lends itself to serious religious distortion. Professor Bernard Anderson in his remarkable book, *Rediscovering the Bible* (p. 179), puts this point provocatively when he says: "apart from the Old Testament the New Testament quickly becomes a non-Christian book". I admit that those words are rather startling. The truth in them is that without the Old Testament Christianity is often interpreted in mystical or non-historical terms. The Bible has its center in Christ. We need not insist that all of its parts help us to understand that center. We must resist the tendency to force all parts of the Bible into a unified Christological pattern. But, as a whole, the Bible is about the revelation of God that has its fulfillment in Christ.

Even after we have located the center of the Bible, it is important to make clear that the revelation is not to be identified with the book or with any part of the book. The Bible points to the revelation. It is a human book about the acts of God. I have been helped in understanding this by a very simple analogy suggested by Bishop Nygren of Sweden. He compared the revelation in Christ to the liberation of Norway from the Nazis. When people in Scandinavia heard of that event it changed the face of the world for them. They heard of it through the radio and the press but these were not the liberating event. They merely pointed to it. The Bible as a book has the same general function as those radio and newspaper reports. It tells us what we know about the events which have indeed changed the face of the world for all mankind.

2. Now I shall turn to the second question—the question concerning the relation of the Bible to the Church. The Bible as a book is the product of the Church. The Church decided what was to be included in the canon. It received the Old Testament as scripture making the decision to reject the Marcionite heresy which would have limited the Bible to a portion of the New Testament. New Testament studies in recent decades give great emphasis to the fact that the New Testament is a book of the Church. Even the gospels consist of materials which the Church found useful in its preaching and teaching.

The deeper truth, however, is that the Bible as a book and the Church itself are both the result of what God has done through persons and events about which we read in the Bible. The revelation that comes to us through the Bible is prior to the Church and is authoritative for the Church. As Canon Wedel has put it, "The Bible as book appeared within the Fellowship. It is, therefore, true to say that the Fellowship came first. The Fellowship was responsible for the Book. But the Fellowship is also responsible to the book, for the Book contains the living Word of God to man." (*The Coming Great Church,* p. 99).

Protestantism differs from all forms of Catholicism in its insistence that the Church must always remain under the revelation that is known through the Bible. There is incalculable importance in the fact that the contemporary Church confronts the Word of God in the Bible as another which it cannot control. Karl Barth has stated this with great effect. He says: "If then, apart from the undeniable and singular aliveness of the Church, there exists over against it a concrete authority with a singular aliveness of its own, an authority whose utterance means not a talking by the Church with herself, but a talking to the Church, which compared with the Church may hold the position of a free power and so of a criterion, obviously it must be distinguished precisely by its written scriptural nature from the mere spiritual and oral life of a Church tradition and given a place before it." *(The Doctrine of the Word of God,* pp. 118-119). This is in sharpest contrast to the Roman Catholic methods of supplementing and finally controlling the word of God in the Bible. (While the Eastern Orthodox Communion differs from Protestantism in its conception of the relation of tradition to the Bible, it differs profoundly from Roman Catholicism in its freedom from centralization, in the fact that it does not add to the authoritative tradition by ecclesiastical fiat, in the place it provides for lay participation even in theology, in its emphasis upon the whole body of the Church as distinguished from the hierarchy, in the spiritual and theological freedom that one finds among its great thinkers.)

However there remains a problem for Protestants. They cannot ignore the Catholic argument that the Bible needs interpretation. On the deepest level the revelation itself cannot be seen to be revelation except by men of faith and this means, in practice, by the Church. This is the truth in the Reformers' emphasis on the witness of the Holy Spirit as the final validation of the revelation. Even the lonely individual who rebels against the Church as an institution but who nourishes his soul on the Bible because he finds an authentic word of God there is himself dependent upon the fact that there has been a Christian community that produced, preserved and interpreted the Bible and which directly, or indirectly, had much to do with the moulding of his own mind.

The revelation that comes to us through the Bible requires interpretation in detail as well as the more fundamental response of faith to which I have referred. The place given to the minister as the interpreter of scripture in Protestantism has been very great. Even churches that give little authority to the minister in their polity in practise depend upon him in large part for the interpretation of the Bible. In historic forms of Protestantism the authority of the minister is derived from the assumption that it is the Word of God that he interprets and not his own private opinions. In contemporary Protestantism the influence of the minister as the interpreter of revelation has greatly declined and his authority too often rests on his own religious experience, his own wisdom about life, his own skills as preacher and pastor and educator. He may be very useful as a guide and leader but he does little to solve the problem of authority for Protestants; instead he adds to the confusion.

It is very important that ministers should be set aside to exercise this function of interpretation, to preach the Word of God week after week and in other ways to mediate it to the congregation. If no one were set aside for this function a local church would not be likely to receive the distinctively Christian guidance which it needs. A purely lay Christian community is in special danger of secularization and of becoming a mere reflection of the local culture. On the other hand, the ministers need to be checked by the insight of laymen in order that they may not become a narrow professional group with its own vested interests. The weaving together of ministers and laymen in the government of many denominations is one of the strong points of Protestantism which is in the sharpest contrast with Roman Catholicism.

The minister should not be an echo of his congregation. He should try to discern the Christian truth, often unexpected and even undesired, that comes to those who reflect upon the scripture and upon much that has been taught about Christian truth at other times and in other places. But if he comes to think of himself as having a monopoly of Christian wisdom and if he begins to lord it over his people he needs to be brought under lay criticism. (Fortunately the Bible is open to laymen as well as to ministers!) How ministers and laymen should guide or correct each other cannot be planned in detail in advance. But the spirit of God works through laymen when churches become too narrowly clerical. We should reject any form of polity that systematically quenches the spirit by discouraging this lay initiative in the church's life.

3. Now let us turn to the final question: what is the relation between what is given through both Bible and Church and the insight and faithful response of the individual?

After we have said everything about the claims of the objective sources of authority, at the end of the day each one of us must decide for himself what he is to believe. Even assent to the authority of the Roman Catholic Church must depend upon the decision of the individual. The only person who has no such responsibility of decision is the person brought up in an environment that is so homogeneous that he is not vividly aware of any alternative to the dominant faith.

If we accept the authority of the Bible somewhat in the way I have interpreted it, we must do so because we are convinced that it is true. Those who accept it as true are still left with innumerable open questions which call for decision. One may be helped by the guidance of the Church but again the individual must choose those trends and movements in the Church which seem to be most authentically Christian. A counting of heads in the Church will not help anyone. Nor will the estimation of formal ecclesiastical weight be decisive. We may be influenced by certain ecumenical trends but even there the process of selection puts a great burden of responsibility on the individual. These choices of the persons or groups or movements within the Church that seem to have most promise always involve a double process. We choose and are chosen at the same time. There is an element of sheer accident here that must be honestly faced because if faced it can be in some measure transcended. It undoubtedly will make a difference whether one happens to study in Basel, Chicago, Edinburgh, New York, Cambridge, New Haven, or Zurich. The geography of theology does have its effect on our decisions even though in the constant interchange of theological thought it is partly corrected. My own students read books written in all of those centers, not in order to introduce them to many curious types of theology but to provide them with materials for their own thought.

The individual's decision for Christ and his interpretation of the meaning of the Christian revelation are influenced by the fact that he has learned a great deal about the world from non-Christian sources. He must not warp what he has learned from the sciences to fit some pre-conceived Christian pattern just as he must not make of science the source of his ultimate faith. He must not deny the partial autonomy of many disciplines and areas of experience. He must be open to truth from every source. He will try to think as a Christian about these disciplines and about these areas of experience but not as though he knows the answers in advance as a Christian.

So important is the acknowledgement of sources of truth outside the Christian orbit marked by Bible and Church that I want to press the matter one step further. Often unwelcome pressure on the Church from outside has proved to be necessary to shake it out of quite unholy ruts. I doubt if the Church, either Catholic or Protestant, without such pressure, would ever have accepted fully and ungrudgingly the principle of religious liberty for all citizens in a country. I doubt if the Churches, apart from the pressure upon them of the whole modern democratic revolution, would have come to see as clearly as they see now the Christian reasons for the trend toward social and economic equality in the world. Here, we should avoid the common secular argument for religious liberty on the ground that religious differences are divisive but unimportant and we should avoid a gospel of equality that is based upon a Marxist rather than a Christian conception of man. Correction of the Church from outside is a costly process but it is often necessary, and the Christian who sees truth in these tendencies and movements which may even be hostile to the Church has a responsibility to represent that truth within the Church. The Christian who accepts this responsibility often gets little help from the leaders of the Church at the time but he should associate himself with other Christians who have similar purposes and with them keep those purposes under the correction of the Biblical revelation.

The individual must finally make his own decisions in matters of faith but he does not make them alone. His mind is formed in part by his response to the Christian revelation. This response takes place within some segment of the Christian community. He stands necessarily at a point where these distinctively Christian influences and currents of thought in the world interact. But even there he should not stand alone. He should take counsel with fellow Christians who stand at the same point. He should also be guided by the experience of Christians who at other times and in other cultural situations have faced similar problems. He should be open to truth from all quarters and yet be careful that the criterion by which he judges comes from Christian faith and not from some other and perhaps unrecognized faith. Bishop Aulen, whose book on the Christian Faith has won very wide acceptance in this country outside his own Lutheran communion suggests the spirit of the Christian enquirer when he discusses the general revelation of God in nature and history. He says about Christianity: "On the one hand, it does not establish any limits around divine revelation, but on the other hand, it refuses to recognize any other God than him who reveals himself in Christ". (*The Faith of the Christian Church,* p. 35.)

SUGGESTIONS FOR FURTHER READING

BERNARD ANDERSON, *Rediscovering the Bible* (New York, 1951).

GUSTAF AULEN. *The Faith of the Christian Church* (Philadelphia, 1948).

JOHN BAILLIE and HUGH MARTIN (editors), *Revelation* (New York, 1937). (Especially the chapters by Karl Barth, William Temple and Walter Horton)

KARL BARTH, *The Doctrine of the Word of God* (New York, 1936).

EMIL BRUNNER, *Revelation and Reason* (Philadelphia, 1946).

C. H. DODD, *The Bible Today* (Cambridge, England, 1947).

P. T. FORSYTH, *The Church and the Sacraments* (London, 1949).

DANIEL JENKINS, *Tradition and the Spirit* (Philadelphia, 1952).

JOHN T. McNEILL, *Unitive Protestantism* (New York, 1930).

THE PROTESTANT CREDO

REINHOLD NIEBUHR, "Coherence, Incoherence, and Christian Faith" in *The Journal of Religion* (July, 1951).

RICHARD NIEBUHR, *The Meaning of Revelation* (New York, 1946).

JOHN OMAN, *Vision and Authority* (New York, 1929).

ALAN RICHARDSON, *Christian Apologetics* (New York, 1947).

ALAN RICHARDSON and W. SCHWEITZER (editors), *Biblical Authority for Today* (Philadelphia, 1952).

PAUL TILLICH, *Systematic Theology* (Chicago, 1951).

THEODORE WEDEL, *The Coming Great Church* (New York, 1945).

AN ANTHROPOLOGICAL APPROACH TO THE ORIGINS OF PROTESTANTISM

By

FRANCIS WILLIAM BUCKLER

FRANCIS WILLIAM BUCKLER

Up until his recent retirement (1951), Francis William Buckler has been, since 1925, professor of church history in the Graduate School of Theology, Oberlin College. His academic training began at the University of Cambridge, England (M.A., 1920) and his earlier teaching career was spent in colleges of India. His association with Cambridge continued with a series of lectureship appointments particularly in the field of Oriental studies. His membership has included numerous academic fraternities, such as the Royal Asiatic Society, the American Oriental Society, the Medieval Academy of America, the American Church History Society (president, 1941). Kenyon College honored him with a Doctor of Sacred Theology degree in 1937. His publications have for the most part been centered upon strictly scholarly pursuits, and among scholars in his field he holds a place of high prestige. Besides technical articles in professional publications he has authored "The Epiphany of the Cross" (1938). He represents the unique combination that exists among many Episcopalian leaders of thought, the compatibility of an Anglican faith with the astutest form of scholarly inquiry. As an historian he reveals the mark of the research mind by his keen imaginative insight into facts, his loyalty to them in spite of layers of traditional theories and his bold acclaim of whatever such facts seem to reveal. His interpretation of Protestantism is important because of just this combination of scholar and loyal churchman.

Editor

AN ANTHROPOLOGICAL APPROACH TO THE ORIGINS OF PROTESTANTISM

Francis William Buckler

A MAJOR injury that has befallen the history of Protestantism has arisen from the limitation of its treatment to the sixteenth century, despite the work of scholars in the fields of Wyclif and Hus, and earlier times. There is, too, another kindred defect, arising from the tendency to treat the Reformation as merely an ecclesiastical movement, whereas it was much more an anthropological development of considerable geographical interest. The trouble dates from the assumption of the universality of Roman (and Western Mediterranean) thought. In other words, there has always been a tendency to transform Christianity from an Oriental barbarian concept of Kingship to a Hellenistic religious concept of a sacrificial order and a norm of ethical conduct within the bounds—or bonds— of Jewish and Graeco-Roman ethical systems. It is at least to the credit of Pilate that he recognized a greater significance, as will appear later. Nor were the malice of the priesthood nor the treason of Judas Iscariot as simple as they appear superficially, even in the Gospels or the Acts. Indeed, the passage from the New Testament to the earliest records of the Church is not an easy one, so much so that the centre of gravity of early Church History passes from Asia and its Achaemenid *milieu, i.e.,* from the lands of the Barbarians, to the lands and colonies of the Graeco-Roman world; from the lands of the Barbarians of the Orient—to the alien atmosphere of Plato, Aristotle and the Stoics in the realm of thought, and of Caesar and the Roman Emperors in the realm of rule. There is a further complication. With the limitation of the frontiers of the Roman Empire to the Rhine, and the Danube in the West,

[141]

one region of expansion was cut off from the field of historical interest, namely, the area of the labours of St. Paul and his
disciples. It can hardly have been mere accident that Martin
Luther's reading of the *Epistle to the Galatians after* his visit
to Rome should have produced the profound change of outlook which ensued, both in faith and churchmanship.

Furthermore, the path to a valid appreciation of the nature
of the Reformation has not been cleared by the stress laid on
the Augustinian common denominator of Luther and Calvin,
for the result is a tendency—at least—to overlook the contrast of Luther's essentially German outlook and Calvin's
essentially Latin point of view, the Augustinian common denominator to the contrary notwithstanding. By the traditional
Protestant cleric as well as by the modern historian, the limitation of the Roman Empire by the three rivers—the Rhine,
the Danube and the Euphrates—has been passed over with
little or no consideration of its historical consequences in its
effects on the policy and point of view of both Roman and
Barbarian. These can be seen both in the lines of Barbarian
attacks and of Roman defence against Barbarian encroachment,
a defence which is the forerunner of the missionary policy of
Gregory the Great and the struggle for Roman papal control
as envisaged in the policy of the clerical party of the Middle
Ages, be it the missionary policy of Gregory the Great or the
internal ecclesiastical policy of Nicholas I and Gregory VII
and their successors. The feud between the Empire and the
Papacy is really the legacy of the feud between Julius Caesar
and Ariovistus, (a name, incidentally, reminiscent of the Persian name Ardabihist).

Another preliminary note is found in the *Epistle to the Galatians*. Galatia forms the northern part and controls the
northern shore of Asia Minor. Its inhabitants were in close
communication with the northern coast of the Black Sea and
particularly the sea of Azov, a region, too, of exile of Byzan-
tine offenders and heretics. The sea of Azov had also been an
area dominated by the Scyths as was northern Asia Minor; for

the Scyths, starting from Asia spread westward to the north and south of Asia Minor where they dominated the territory and city of Tarsus, and spread over Syria and Palestine as far as the desert, leaving a memorial of their occupation in the city called Scythopolis. There seems little reason to doubt, therefore, that if the Mediterranean had become a Roman lake by the time of Augustus, the area represented by the lands from the Persian Gulf to the North Sea along the northern and eastern frontiers of the Roman Empire had become Scythian under a variety of tribal names. The process dates from the seventh century B.C. and is not seriously impeded despite occasional reverses in wars against the Romans, as the Scyths were moving westward under pressure from the advancing Slavs. Furthermore they are akin to the Indo-Iranian, and so to the Indo-Germanic stock.

Between the Scythian and Germanic peoples there appears to have been a considerable amount of amalgamation for the name of Wodan is simply a form of the Scythian *Khwadā-nathān,* as Anquetil Duperron discovered as long ago as 1788 and the word is connected with the idea of the divine and royal Glory. It is found in the Iranian name Kubād or Kuwād (Kai Kobad) ; it also appears in Hebrew *Ha Kavōd Yahwēh,* a legacy from the Captivity. Furthermore it is associated with fire or great light. (Handel's *Messiah* is in many ways the best western exposition of the idea available to the ordinary Western reader, and none can deny the German Handel's grasp of its implicit idea.) Furthermore, there is the participial form *Wodanāz,* which contains the three principal root consonants. There are ceremonial parallels too: the words of Caiaphas, "It is fitting that one man die and the people perish not" (Jn. xi.50, xviii.14), as well as by the hostile critic of the neighbours of the Jews, "Cursed is he who is hanged on a tree" (Deut. xxi.23; *cf.* Gal. iii.13). The second example is the text: (i) the allusion of St. Peter: "The God of our fathers raised up Jesus, whom ye slew and hanged on a tree" (Acts v.30; *cf.* x.39). If this verse has any significance at all, it is an ironical allusion to the so-called Crucifixion by which the Kingdom of God had been ushered in. This royal sacrifice is implicit in the account of the death of the German Arminius in Tacitus. The date of his death was 20 A.D., and there is no reason for regarding it as the sole or the first occasion of that form of death on a tree. Furthermore "crucifixion" was a Roman form of execution, but hanging on a tree was a barbarian form of royal sacrifice, recorded (or noticed) by Herodotus, Tacitus and others. The man destined to hang on the tree, whether Arminius in Germany or Jesus in Judaea, was King, as recognized by Pontius Pilate, who had probably served in Germany as well as Judaea; and as St. Paul's teaching implied, for it implies justification by faith in the king as well as belief in the good faith of the sufferer and the God he represents. It lies at the heart of Kingship—or "Kingdom". Inasmuch as the quest of justification by works impugns the validity and finality of the royal sacrifice or pride in him who maintains his self-sufficiency by failing to ascribe the glory of his own works to God, it is doubly anathema. It was this faith, representing *German* Christianity, which produced the sneer of Boniface of Mainz in reference to the German Christians who refused to accept *his* teaching. It was not surprising, however, (though he might have known better) for from the northern boundary of Tibet westwards, there runs a dividing line to the shores of the Atlantic: it is the boundary between the peoples who call the supreme deity *Khwadā-nathān,* God, *Gott, Khuda, Khshatra, Shah,* and those who call him *Theos, Deus, Dieu, Dios;* it corresponds with the division between King, *König,* and *Raja, rex* and *roi.* The difference is again primarily the difference between the Scythian roots and the Indian (and Mediterranean) characteristics.

There is yet another set of factors necessary for a full assessment of the emergence of Luther's faith. His early life was spent amid the 'paganism' of north Germany, and he never forgot this faith, despite the attitude of his father, despite the struggles reflected, perhaps in the lines:

> And though this world with devils filled
> Shall threaten to o'erwhelm us.

His mother was a believer in local superstitions, and his father scoffed at the teaching of the Church. It is this collection of facts, culminating in the strong note of Sacramental Kingship, which marks his teaching, that calls for revision of the customary view of Germanic Protestantism, along with a certain elusiveness when attempts are made to align it with other forms produced by the Reformation. Luther marks a rebellion not only against Catholic theology but also against the classical Renaissance and Mediterranean and by this fact he is differentiated from Calvin, who never departed from the path marked out for him by his classical education and legal training. In this respect, Calvin represents Mediterranean Latinity while Luther's teaching represented Baltic Germany, and his influence has persisted only in areas where the classical Renaissance did not emerge triumphant. The contrast might be summed up by a literary parody: Calvin was a theological Brutus—

> The noblest Roman of them all—

in open rebellion against a Roman ecclesiastical tyrannos but none the less, a Roman lawyer; Luther was a Christian Arminius, fighting the ecclesiastical successor of his predecessor's foes.

It is this setting which suggests the reasons for much of the hostile criticism—even by Protestants—of Luther's activities during the later years of his life, and the desirability of a reassessment of the German Reformation, and, with it, of the whole of Germanic Christianity, but particularly the status of the cult of Wodan.

In the traditional form in which Anglo-Saxon and Germanic history are presented, Wodan is treated as the heathen god, whose worship precedes the conversion to Christianity. It is the validity of this view that it is the object of this paper to examine.

The most convenient starting point is the episode of the death of Agrippa (44 A.D.), recorded fully by Josephus, but only in mangled form in the Acts. When he "was standing in bonds and leaning on a tree on which sat an owl, a *German* prisoner, having obtained permission of his guard to speak to him, pointed out the bird to Agrippa, and informed him that he was shortly to be released and to be promoted to kingship, but that when he saw the bird again he would know that he had but five days to live. The sequel occurred in the third year of his reign, when he exhibited spectacles in Caesar's honour.

"On the second day of the performances he entered the theatre at daybreak, arrayed in a wonderfully woven robe made entirely of silver; whereupon the silver caught by the first rays of the sun, was lit up and glittered in a marvellous manner, with dazzling flashes that struck terror and awe into the onlookers. His flatterers straightway ... raised cries, which even to him seemed ill-omened, calling him a god. . . . The King neither rebuked them nor rejected their impious adulation; but not long after he looked up and saw the owl sitting on a rope above his head and at once recognized the former bringer of good tidings as now the messenger of ill. Five days later he was dead". (*Cf. Acts*, xii. 21-23.)

Midway between the death of Arminius (20 A.D.) and the death of Herod (44 A.D.) lies the death of Jesus of Nazareth, "the King of the Jews", and, like that of Arminius, also on a tree (Acts v, 30, x. 39). Furthermore, Herod's attempt to seize the Glory, "which cannot be captured by force or fraud" is reflected in a statement by St. Paul, (unfortunately mistranslated "changed" instead of "invested", not unto death, as in the case of Herod, but unto life [1. Cor., xv. 52-54]). The association of the Glory with the sea or a lake stretches from the Bay of Bengal to the Baltic and the Atlantic, nor does the Mediterranean escape, for the *pallium* is worn by the Pope at the Mass of the Fisherman which precedes the investiture of a papal legate which is Latin for *Khalīfah* (caliph) or deputy. On that occasion, the Pope sits on the throne of the Fisherman. The important point to be noticed, however, is that there is a common bond between Palestine, Syria and Asia Minor, as the Western provinces of the realm of the King of kings, and the northern coast of the Euxine Sea; furthermore, there is the movement of the peoples, particularly the Scythians, who partly forced the Germanic peoples westward or partly amalgamated with them. They also moved in a south-westerly direction into Cilicia (whose capital is Tarsus), Syria and Palestine, in the wake of their frustrated attempt to conquer Egypt. In Palestine they founded a city Skythopolis to the north of Jerusalem. They also left traces of their influence as far north-west as Scotland, where the Scythian word *breeks* remains a living verbal monument to their influence.

Along this path appear traces of all the essential marks of the royal sacrifice: the death of the King on the tree. It should not be overlooked that when the High Priest said "It is fitting that one man die and the people perish not", he proclaimed the Victim as King; and Pilate, who possibly (even probably) had witnessed and certainly had heard of the death of Arminius in A.D. 20, proceeded officially, after a private talk with Jesus, to order the epitaph, "Jesus of Nazareth, the King of the Jews" to be affixed to the tree on which He was hanged, and refused either to modify or to remove it, when the Jewish authorities protested.

What Pilate had refused to do became the function and duty of the Church Fathers of Mediterranean Christianity in its opposition to Barbarian intrusions into the faith. From Marcion, Arius and Nestorius onwards, Hellenistic metaphysical canons of philosophical soundness, combined with Roman demands for ecumenical orthodoxy and a common standard of theological terminology militated against all attempts to present the Christ *as the anointed King,* and the concept of Sonship was exploited metaphysically to the full. The victims extend from Paul of Samosata to Theodore of Mopsuestia and Nestorius, all of whom have a common Oriental background independent of any Judaistic leanings. Chaos became worse confounded until Justin and his nephew sought a new solution to the problem of Christian doctrinal unity. Justinian's theological position, therefore, takes on a significance far beyond the scant respect paid to it by theologians, for it marks the last intervention of barbarian theological influence in the Mediterranean area prior to the inroads of Islam and the obliteration of Christian strength from Persia, the Middle East, North Africa, to Spain and France. It also cut off the Scytho-Germans of the North from Mediterranean influences, except such as entered by way of France or the passes to the north of Venice. The southern advance of the Turk completed the work of the advance of the Slavs to their north, and it is only in relatively recent years that the task of reducing to historical order the chaos of this region has been seriously attacked.

It is necessary now to turn to the cult of Wodan, as it appears to combine two significant strands of Christian thought prior to their emergence as individual and mutually exclusive heresies—Nestorianism and Theopaschitism.

Nestorius was a learned Persian Christian, whose father had been forced to flee from his native land on account of persecutions, and the position he took in the question of the Person of Christ and the relation of the divine to the human was fundamentally simple: when the face of the Son is turned towards the Father, the Son is human; when His face is turned towards man, it is the face of the Divine. As the Greek for the face is *prosōpon,* and the divine and the human were joined, so to speak, there, this relationship was called *prosōpic union.* Here, Nestorius shows perfectly soundly the position of the King, and, even more, the working of the Kingdom of God on earth in the Person of the Son, but, most important, he envisages the Atonement with a finality and simplicity elsewhere unsurpassed. Nestorius was a Barbarian, however, and it was still fitting that the Greeks rule—or excommunicate—the Barbarians.

The other doctrine, the Theopaschite heresy, that God suffered on the Cross is of still greater interest, as already noticed, inasmuch as it reproduced the reality of the cult of Wodan. The form is revealed in the formula of the sacrifice,

Self unto myself

or 'given of myself to myself'. The literary monument to this cult is St. Paul's *Epistle to the Galatians*. It is significant that Tarsus in Cilicia had been under the influence of the Scythians prior to its conquest by the Romans. Furthermore the note "self unto myself" is characteristic of and implicit in both Pauline and Joannine theology, and it is the point of departure of both from the views of James and the Synoptists' tradition. There is a curious commentary on this point in the correspondence of Boniface of Mainz. His letters contain no reference to St. Paul except to the bridge and church in Rome named after him. On the other hand, the literary monument to Scythian Christianity is the Epistle to the Galatians, which re-emerges in Martin Luther's commentary. The consequence is significant: the form "self unto myself" emerges naturally from "given of myself" when once the doctrine of the divinity of "the Son" becomes axiomatic and is cut off from the area of Nicene, and Christological controversy. It is equally significant that Justinian I, despite earlier opposition to the formula in c.534, was ultimately convinced and was able to carry it in 553 A.D. Under his pressure it was accepted by Pope Vigilius, who forfeited thereby his right to burial in St. Peter's.

There is an important sequel to the subsequent division of the area of Wodan from the Roman area, noticed as early as the eighteenth century by Anquetil Duperron and published with additional material by Burnouf in 1829. They pointed out the high ancestry of the form Guodan, preserved by Paul the Lombard, and its sequel in the sixteenth century. There are two ancient words for the name or title of the Deity: *Khuda*, which is akin to God or Gott, and Deva, which becomes Theos, Deus, Dieu in the West. It is not without significance that the Evangelical Reformation succeeded only among the peoples using the form God and its various forms, *e.g.,* Germany, England, Scotland, Holland and Scandinavia. This division was emphasized by the spread of Islam and the advance of the Slavs, which combined to cut off the communications of the Germanic North from the Mediterranean South. It is marked by the rise of the Germanic Empire *vis-à-vis* "the Ghost of the Roman Empire seated enthroned on the tomb thereof", and the obliteration of the ancient centres of Christian missions by Slav and Saracen, crowned by the triumph of the Ottoman Turk in the fifteenth and sixteenth centuries.

Northern Germany succeeded in maintaining groups of Christians, whose faith was despised by the Roman Church as "differing but little from the surrounding heathenism". The words of Boniface of Mainz. Among the earliest objects of attack was the date of Easter. The account of the controversy given by Bede is not an elevating story but the record of ecclesiastical chicanary in alliance with royal stupidity and selfishness. It is a Roman triumph, but it was unable to kill Anglo-Saxon faith, which appears triumphant in "The Dream of the Rood", the brightest gem of Anglo-Saxon literature. It is in this area, which includes Holland and North Western Germany, and is sufficiently removed from Mediterranean ecclesiastical control, where the faith of the Cross—or Rood— persists; and it is from these regions that the *soi-disant* Reformation begins: the Saxons and their kin in Germany, Britain and Scandinavia who have maintained this faith in Him, *who was hanged on a Tree.* The distance from Wodan and Germanic Catholic Christianity is marked by the contrast between *The Dream of the Rood* and the emergence of the Mediterranean doctrine of the Real Presence, which finds its culmination in the doctrine of Transubstantiation.

The second main strand of the Reformation, represented chiefly by Calvin, is essentially Latin in mood. If Luther represents the German mood of Arminius, Calvin represents the mood of Cato and the Roman Republic or an ecclesiastical

Brutus attacking the imperial pretensions of an Alexander VI or Julius II. The classical Renaissance was the Mediterranean counterpart of the transalpine 'national' movements. Consequently the mood of Calvin's attack on the Renaissance Papacy is classical in form and spirit, and destiny or fate are the marks of inscrutable divine will and supremacy. Submission, therefore, becomes the supreme virtue—and necessity. Like Luther, Calvin marks an appeal from the Latin Church to the "Greatest of the Latin Fathers", St. Augustine. Neither believed in the freedom of the will, though in Luther's theology the mood was Germanic and heroic, Calvin's view was Latin and precise, and did not extend the benefits of grace to the heretic.

In another respect the two differed: Calvin was a Roman republican while Luther was a German royalist. Here the contemptuous gibe that Luther put his trust in *princes principes* serves only to obscure the significance of his real contribution. The princes of the Holy Roman Empire were the Kings of its constituent people. The King was the man anointed to die that the people perish not; the word is Germanic: the "prince" *(princeps)* is a word of *Latin* origin, and refers primarily to supreme military command and leadership of the army—*one* of the functions of the king retained by a people who had caused their kings to flee and celebrated the anniversary of the *regi fugium* (royal flight) as their Independence Day. Consequently the underlying note of his concept of the Kingdom of God is founded upon a rigid determinism which, coupled with divine absolutism, produces the doctrine of predestination usually associated with his name. There is nothing new in the concept, for what emerges is simply Jove, cleansed of his amorous peccadilloes, to appear in virtuous sternness of an eclectic moral order, carrying with it the arbitrary sentence of predetermined salvation or damnation. The revival of the concept of the *patria potestas* (and the Roman grimness thereunto appertaining) produced a deity of power undiluted, save for the few, who were destined to heavenly bliss. It was this element of grim sternness which gave to Calvinism and Calvinists their power to resist persecution and oppression, and the effect is seen most clearly in the periods of Catholic purging: it is generally held that Calvinist renegades were rare but Lutherans easily submitted to the demand for conformity. Such a statement is as difficult to attest as to rebut and the writer of this chapter lays no claim to the right of adjudication. In modern parlance, what Calvin provided was "the machine" to break the Counter-Reformation, and it stood the test of The Thirty Years War. In the subsequent Industrial Revolution it gained a further victory in the economic field, but perhaps its most ironical triumph emerges in the gift of a Cardinal's hat to the erstwhile Calvinist, John Henry Newman, who owed both his moral Latinity and severity, not to the Church of Rome, which, moreover brought him but little comfort or satisfaction, but to his father's austere Low Church Puritanism.

*　　*　　*　　*　　*　　*

Protestantism, in one of its aspects at least, then, can be regarded as evidence of the realization by the Western nations of their full right to emancipation from external dictation as to the form or content of their national faith. Rome had overplayed her hand in the cases of Henry IV of Germany and even of King John in England, particularly in the sequel of the reign of Henry III. The climax was reached in the reigns of Henry VIII and Elizabeth I, when the unity and the safety of the realm appeared to be threatened not merely from within but also from without. The defeat of the Spanish Armada in 1588 belongs as much to Church History as to naval history; the outburst of thankful relief was a genuine religious outburst, and, as a Spanish victory would have prepared the way for the annexation of Scotland, the union of the two kingdoms was henceforth inevitable. The situation recurred in the reign of James II, and the Anglo-Dutch alliance to check the victorious career of Louis XIV was the next great triumph of Protestantism. The sequel was the advent of the Elector of

Hanover as George I and the dynasty which still occupies the British throne. The tragedy of the wars between the two great Germanic nations lies not least in the commentary of Catholic and Communist advances within Protestant areas. As already noticed, Charles the Great regretted the coronation of Christmas, 800, and always maintained that had he known the intention of Leo III, he would never have entered the church that Christmas Day. His subsequent conduct towards the Pope proved it. The Anglo-German feud has split the core of Protestantism and the various metamorphoses of Holy Leagues and Leagues of Nations have not proved able to stay the religio-diplomatic deterioration.

This last point throws some light on diplomatic and ecclesiastical developments. It should never be forgotten that the German proclamation of the imperial status of the King of Prussia in 1871 was intended as a step taken towards the undoing of the mischief of Christmas Day, 800. The point that it served as a diplomatic reply to the pronouncement of Papal infallibility as well as an assertion of Prusso-German pride should not be overlooked. Nor should sympathy with the French be permitted to hide the fact. It is no answer to reply that French religious feeling was at a low ebb, for Gallicanism has always been the basis of the French "Munro Doctrine". The subsequent rise of Papal claims against Protestant areas, and the effect of the anti-Hitler understandings with the Vatican, have led to a marked recession in Protestant strength and courage. Furthermore, subsequent developments in the movements towards Christian Unity are fraught with considerable danger and anxiety. Rome harassed the Germanic revival, which had been started by the Carolingian House (even to the extent of crowning Charles as Emperor, none the less no word of protest against Hitler or Mussolini's atrocities came from the Vatican, and the ruthless attack on Ethiopian [heretics] was, if not approved openly, given tacit consent).

In the reigns of Charles V and Philip II, and the Spanish threat combined with the activities of the Jesuits, was the menace of the reign of Elizabeth I. The Spanish Armada, combined with the Spanish policy in the Netherlands, was as important a development of the Counter-Reformation as the Thirty Years War, which broke out thirty years later; in fact it was Britain's contribution to the struggle for the safety of Protestantism. The Franco-Prussian War split the Gallican-German core of the strength of the opponents to Pseudo-Isidorian developments and paved the way for the subsequent disasters which have split the Protestant world and strength in face of the dual attack from Rome and Moscow, at a time when the diplomatic maps of Europe resembled the map of the *Volkerwanderung* (wandering of the peoples), more than it has in any period since the coronation of Charles the Great.

Protestantism, consequently, has gained a new significance in its external aspects. As a Christian faith, it is called upon to face and oppose the political and national religious creeds of both Rome and Russia even as it found it had to face the *nazionale* movement of Hitler; as the form of faith of the Barbarian peoples, it is brought into direct opposition to Catholicism. It has therefore been driven to attempt the discovery of means of union within its own fold in face of an increase in the hostile forces ranged against its churches. This has been particularly true of the mission field, which has been brought into the arena of nationalist struggles accompanied by a conservative revival of national against exotic religions. The point of attack is generally the complicated metaphysical statements of the creeds, as well as a variety of ethical criticisms. The Christian communities have usually maintained their faith, even in face of persecution, but the question still remains: How long can this persist without refreshment from outside?

To meet this need Protestant Churches have been forced to adopt a conciliar movement of their own in favour of Christian Reunion. Their object so far has been to discover the greatest common denominator of agreement. This path, though probably the only obvious one, has served in the main to reveal the high degree of intractability within the area of any individual church's creed as well as the elements of national or ecclesiastical pride. The case of German protestantism, whether in Germany or America, ranges from extreme Lutheranism (Evangelical) to extreme Calvinistic (Reformed) with the slight margin of agreement in the Evangelical-Reformed Church; similarly the Episcopal discipline, ranging from the Orthodox Church to Methodism. Even within its own orbit, union has proved difficult in each of the categories, and joint-services do not appear to have been very effective as a means towards Reunion. The question, then, still remains: How can Protestantism face the challenge of Catholicism in the matter of unity? There is, however, a further question: "Should it, even if it could?"

The contributor of this paper firmly believes that the true answer is in the negative, on the basis of the axiom above, "He that will seek to save his life shall lose it". The inherent danger of movements towards ecclesiastical mergers lies in the high probability of mere verbal compromise in difficult cases. It is impossible to read the history of the doctrine of the Person of Christ down to the reign of Justinian I without realizing the force of the text: "He that shall seek to save his life, —or point,—shall lose it". By substituting "unity" for "life" it is possible to read the lesson of Church History on this point. Dogmatic integrity is no valid substitute for Christian conviction, tolerance and charity, for ultimately the implication of Protestantism is "Justification by faith", and faith is either the product of or the ratio between the individual and the satisfaction of his need, be it spiritual or physical. It is the pragmatist who demands justification by works, whatever their form or type, and the Devil was the first pragmatist (as "The Temptations" teach), though he has been followed by Church Councils ever since. For Pragmatism is the denial of faith and its existence in force today; both in Church and State its strength calls for the revival of the two leading doctrines of Protestantism: Justification by Faith and belief in Divine supremacy—for the good of the individual man—the son of man, in face of the evil doctrine of the Prince of this World, —or justification by works, or, more briefly, efficiency, which can be summed up as

> Ever striving but never able to come to the knowledge of the truth.

*   *   *   *   *   *

In this short sketch of Protestantism an attempt has been made to find and test a new evaluation of its origin and characteristics not from any preconceived concept of superiority of churchmanship, ethical standards or methods of worship, but as the expression of faith of the Germanic peoples. The attempt has been based on the historical possibility and probability of its representing a continuation of the feud between St. Paul and St. Peter. The writer has something more than doubt that St. Peter was ever in Rome, but believes that he ended his life in 'the other Babylon', whither he appears to have gone after his quarrel with St. Paul. He is also personally convinced, though it cannot be finally proved, that the episode of Simon Magus (and still more the developments of the story in the *Clementines*) represents the anti-Pauline propaganda of the Petrine party after the quarrel between the two Apostles. If that is so, the Petrine claims to infallibility take on a new complexion, and, with it, the disdain of German native Christianity, shown by the ultramontane Boniface of Mainz and his successors, is not to be taken lightly. "The Dream of the Rood" discloses an atmosphere of thought nearer to the Cross than it is to "orthodox" Christianity, even prior to the outbreak of the "Investiture contest", and the subsequent struggle between German and Roman versions of the faith. It also gives force to the status of Royal Supremacy, whether in France, Germany, England or Scotland.

The reason for this recapitulation is the need to keep in the foreground the views which were smothered by the use of the Latin language as the mediaeval *lingua franca*. It has its parallels elsewhere, for instance, the Indian reversion to the native languages against the compulsory use and learning of English in schools and colleges The Reformation was the fore-runner of the outburst of vernacular literature from the spirit shown in the *Nibelungenlied* to the Elizabethan and Stuart outburst of English literature. It is possible to carry this point still farther. It was this spirit which gave full vitality to secular representative government and the coming of age of Parliament under Henry VIII and Elizabeth I.

This side of the work of the Reformation is as important as any religious or ecclesiastical contribution, and must not be ignored as a mere secular sphere, for the emancipation of the Church from the unnatural limitations of celibacy of the clergy brought the Christian life from its spectacular aloofness from the "laity",—or the son of man,—back again into human life and into contact with its reality, as in the words and mood of the hymn,

> The daily round, the common task
> Will furnish all we need to ask
> Room to deny ourselves, a road
> To bring us daily nearer God.

If this, and not the theological wrangling of cleric and theologian, is the final analysis of the meaning of Protestantism, Protestantism may be in danger, but it is not yet dead. The Nietzschean note was seen by J. N. Figgis, and in order to render intelligible the words "I have come that ye might have life and have it abundantly," Nietzsche had to call it the gospel of Anti-Christ, though his scorn of Luther was not a just judgment, it was the corollary to the *Pietists'* Luther, which is still the bane of the historical Luther, for there is, as Thomas Carlyle noticed, by his inclusion in *Heroes and Hero Worship*, a place for him among the heroes at a time best described by the poem

> Once to every man and nation
> Comes the moment to decide.

It is the moment which reveals the Hero's decision to renounce (deny) himself to the uttermost, even to death, and so to reveal himself in his glory,—the glory of death on a tree, that his people may have life. There is no escape from the Christology implicit.

* * * * * *

If the validity of the foregoing assessment of the bases of the *Protestant Credo* be granted, the question emerges, "What will be the final form and content of the emergent Protestant Credo? How far will the formulae of the Ancient Creeds of Christendom, weighed down by ecclesiastical conciliar pronouncement as they are, succeed in meeting the new situation? What are the defects which need to be overcome, and can they be overcome?"

The first point to be noticed, it may be fairly stated, is that the source of the historical Creeds would appear to be medicinal and empirical. They emerge as confessions of orthodox faith, framed in terms of rebuttal of contemporary heresy, be it doctrinal or ecclesiastical, and all tend to conform to the formula:

"Inasmuch as it seemed good unto the Holy Ghost, *and to us*". In modern times Neander was probably the first Church Historian to recognize this factor; the new ecumenical conciliarists, however, have tended to hold to the content, discarding the brevity of the pre-Tridentine *formulae*.

The function of the *Credo* of a church is the enunciation of the terms of its faith with a brevity which renders memorization possible; with a simplicity and clarity, which can be understood by all entitled to utter it; in terms and wording which are accurate in their description, with proper regard for the limitations of their application. Within the Church Catholic, as well as the Churches national or 'schismatic', the basis of form is to be found in the Apostles' Creed and its derivatives, whether doctrinal or historical. Other Churches, mainly those which have emerged from Pietist groups of the period of the

Reformation, have rejected creeds, on grounds either of doctrine or fitness for a place in worship. In others, the place of the creed is little more than a definition of the terms of admission to membership of the Church. The word *Credo,* however has a more personal note than the derivative "Creed" contains—a note which it is essential to keep alive. Therein lies the *sine qua non* of some formulation of a Creed. The Creeds of Mediterranean origin have set the form of the historic creeds of most Churches, and are philosophical, Patristic and Synoptic in form and content. It is frequently maintained that their object is rather the exclusion of error than the exposition of truth and that they are not Christian, inasmuch as they tend towards formal and vain repetition.

There is no doubt of an element of truth in the allegation. Nevertheless, the fact remains that the ordinary human being needs and desires some formal statement, opening with the formal expression "I believe", without philosophical terms of doubtful validity in his own day. The parallel basis of Hellenistic philosophical form and expression of the first four centuries would be represented to-day by one of atomic speculation! In both fields the ordinary layman is bound to be led astray, homiletic instruction to the contrary notwithstanding.

On the other hand, Churches which have dispensed with the use of formal statements of a creed have not necessarily escaped from the evils which they assign to the nature of Creeds, particularly the two historic Creeds of Western Christendom, but their case does not concern us as the term *Credo* (as a noun) has gradually come to mean the personal belief of an individual, whether verbally formulated or remaining in a state of suspension, to such a degree that its expression is mainly negative, summed up in the formula ascribed to Jowett:—"I used to believe".

The main function of the *Credo,* as distinct from the "Creed" in its classic (or patristic) form is that it is primarily positive, in that it aims at the inclusion of all that is necessary to be believed in order to confess membership of "the body of Christ". Inasmuch as the status of Him, who was hanged on a tree in Jerusalem, was that of a King,—the King of the Jews, as Pilate insisted,—hence any *Credo* to be valid must be framed in terms of kingship and allegiance, and not limited to a mere series of theological definitions. It must include recognition of them who, by virtue of their own sacrifice, have become the Christs of their own Christ, and so members of His Body, by virtue of their part as His deputies. In order to find the proper definition and term, it is necessary to turn away from the Mediterranean languages of Greek and Latin to the modern Semitic language of the Near East. They become the Caliphs of the Caliph of God, inasmuch as they have accepted His cast-off 'Garment', (the Cross of Shame), as their Robe of His Glory.

The essence of a Protestant *Credo* must be emancipation from the shackles of Mediterranean philosophy, usage, law and jurisdiction, be it Greek, Roman or Judaistic, for the earthly status of Jesus was that of The True Khalifah—successor—of Cyrus the Great, the King of Kings of his age, as set forth by the Second Isaiah,—and Handel's "Hallelujah Chorus".

SUGGESTIONS FOR FURTHER READING

A. BARCLAY, *The Protestant Doctrine of the Lord's Supper: a Study in the Eucharistic Teaching of Luther, Zwingli and Calvin* (Glasgow, 1927).

J. BITHELL (editor), *Germany, A Companion to German Studies* (London, 1932).

H. M. CHADWICK, *The Cult of Wodan* (Cambridge, 1899).

——, *The Heroic Age* (Cambridge, 1912).

R. E. DAVIES, *The Problem of Authority in the Continental Reformers: A study in Luther, Zwingli and Calvin* (London, 1946).

J. N. FIGGIS, *The Divine Right of Kings* (2nd Ed.) (Cambridge, 1914).

R. K. GORDON, *Anglo-Saxon Poetry* (*Everyman*), (London, 1926).

J. MACKINNON, *Luther and the Reformation* (London, 1928).

——, *Calvin and the Reformation* (London, 1936).

A. F. POLLARD, *Factors in Modern History* (London, 1932).

——, *Cranmer and the English Reformation* (London, 1904).

J. R. TANNER, *Constitutional Documents, A. D. 1485-1603. With historical commentary* (Cambridge, 1930).

R. H. TAWNEY, *Religion and the Rise of Capitalism* (London, 1926).

The Cambridge Modern History, Volume II, (The Reformation) (Cambridge, 1903).

THE PROMISE OF PROTESTANTISM —
WHITHER AND WHETHER
By
HENRY NELSON WIEMAN

Henry Nelson Wieman

If a reader is looking for an account of religion that is preeminently philosophical in approach he will do well to read the works of Henry Nelson Wieman. The essay in this volume is no exception. By philosophical we mean reflective, independent and genuinely creative thinking. For many years now Professor Wieman's name has been at the top-level of those whose writings have inspired genuinely fresh thinking upon old themes. Among his many well known books are: "Religious Experience and the Scientific Method" (1926); "The Wrestle of Religion with Truth" (1927); "Methods of Private Religious Living" (1929); "The Issues of Life" (1931); "Normative Psychology of Religion" (1935); and numerous cooperative volumes. His doctor of philosophy degree was earned at Harvard; his honorary doctor's degrees came from Park College and Occidental College. Besides fulfilling many lectureships he has taught at many American educational institutions. Since 1927 he has been a member of the faculty of the Divinity School of the University of Chicago and now holds the rank of emeritus professor. Since his retirement he has taught in eastern and southern American universities. The importance of his thought has long been recognized. Religion must keep pace with scientific procedure and be refashioned in the light of the best in tested experience and thus become a thing vital to the contemporary age—he has been saying. Protestantism is here interpreted as nourishing the kernel of free, disciplined and creative thinking in the vanguard of Christian progression.

Editor

THE PROMISE OF PROTESTANTISM — WHITHER AND WHETHER

Henry Nelson Wieman

PROTESTANTISM is a beginning not yet completed. It is preparation for a task yet to be done. But like an athlete out of training, it is not ready for the supreme achievement. A revolutionary religious undertaking must be carried through in this age if the human race is to find the way that leads *from* death and destruction and *unto* the best that man can ever become. Protestantism has latent capacities that fit it for this most urgent task. But these capacities must be lifted from their latency and brought into full exercise. Protestantism carries this promise and the time has come to fulfill it.

Protestantism is undisciplined, disorganized, with no clear sense of its mission except the negative sense of being opposed to Roman Catholicism. Its churches often strive to hold an audience by means of folksy talk and light entertainment, or by a fighting campaign against a local evil. Entertainment and fighting campaigns have their place. But the destiny of man and history is at stake and no church is true to its name if it does not hold its people by what it does about this destiny. There is something of compelling importance to present but many church services seem like blasphemy against the background of this awful responsibility.

If other forms of religion are equally endowed with Protestantism for doing the religious task of our time, so be it. But being a Protestant myself, my responsibility is to see what my form of faith can do when it corrects its faults and exercises its capacities to the full. Protestantism has a threefold capacity for the religious task of our time, due to the form of its organization and the content of its teaching.

This threefold capacity of Protestantism is: capacity for unlimited self-criticism, reaching up to the topmost leaders and out into every doctrine and form of practice; capacity for unlimited religious inquiry, no matter what doctrine or cherished belief may be disturbed, providing that the principles of inquiry are followed; capacity for unlimited revolutionary transformation in doctrine, practice and institutional structure, provided that this transformation is demanded by the self-criticism and/or religious inquiry.

Perhaps never in our Christian history of two thousand years has there been such need for the full exercise of these potentialities of Protestantism, and perhaps never before so great an opportunity to exercise them. In this sense the four hundred years since Luther are chiefly a preparation for the constructive work that is now to be done. Many obstacles in the prevalent forms and practices of Protestantism must be overcome or removed before it can do what is now so sorely needed and for which there is so great an opportunity. These obstacles within Protestantism itself may never be overcome and so the promise of Protestantism may never be fulfilled. But the promise is there to be fulfilled if and when these obstacles are removed and the threefold capacity fully exercised.

In the following discussion I shall try to demonstrate the thesis that has been stated. I shall do this by showing, so far as I am able, the following:

1) The need and opportunity in our time for religious self-criticism, religious inquiry and revolutionary transformation.

2) What should be done to meet this need and opportunity.

3) The form of faith in Protestantism which fits it for this task.

I deliberately put in third place my interpretation of Protestantism, after I have set forth the religious need and opportunity of our time and what should be done about it. I have done this because I do not think that Protestantism is important merely because it is Protestantism. It is important only to the measure that it can clear the way and point the path between man and God in a way to meet the religious need and opportunity. Only when we see what is needed religiously, can we interpret and appraise any form of institutional religion in terms that have any importance. Apart from the religious task there is no standard to criticize, appraise and interpret Protestantism. So I first discuss this religious task, then go on to discuss Protestantism in relation to it.

Since it is not uncommon to present Protestantism as the critic and corrective of Catholicism, perhaps I should hasten to state at this point that I think this practice is one of the evils in Protestantism that must be overcome before its high promise can be fulfilled. It is true that the first great Reformers and creators of Protestantism fought the evils of Catholicism; but that was due to the peculiar conditions of their time. In their time there was no institutional form of religion to criticize and correct except that of the Roman Catholic Church. In our time, such is no longer the case. In our time, in the United States at least, the dominant form of institutional religion appears to be Protestantism. If Luther lived in our midst he would fight the evils in Protestantism as much as ever he fought them in Catholicism. Some of his statements uttered in his latter days after various forms of Christianity had arisen outside of the Catholic church would seem to make this evident. In any case, complacency about Protestantism, bitter criticism of Catholicism, and preening ourselves about "the heritage of the Reformation" will make impossible the exercise of that threefold capacity which carries all the high promise of the Protestant form of Christianity.

I

The Need of Our Time

The need of man in our time for religious inquiry, religious self-criticism and religious revolutionary transformation cannot be intelligently considered until we first settle on what is man's religious need in all times. Without settling on this basic, universal need, we have no frame of reference. Any religious need peculiar to our time can only be some modification of this need common to all time.

The religious need of man in all times is to commit himself to what has such extra-human character and power that it can save him from the greatest evils and transform him into the best that human life can ever become, provided that he commits himself to it and meets the other conditions that may be required. This universal religious need springs from man's capacity to be transformed. More than anything else in existence, so far as I know, man can retain the identity of his nature (that of being human) while undergoing extremes of radical transformation. In some of these transformations he becomes a monstrous horror, in others a glorious saint. Extremes of stupidity and extremes of intelligence, extremes of cruelty and extremes of sacrificial love, extremes of helplessness and extremes of power, extremes of suffering and extremes of joy are his. This capacity to undergo extreme transformation and still be a human being is perhaps the most distinctive mark of man.

This capacity to be transformed reveals the deepest need of man. It is to commit himself to what can transform him into the best that he can ever become and avoid commitment to, or exposure to, what will transform him into the monster of evil, horror and suffering that he can also become. In view of these extremes of transformation which man can undergo, the myths of heaven and hell convey a profound truth. Man can be damned; he needs to be saved; he can be lifted to realms of blessedness beyond the reach of any imagination at his command prior to such transformation. The religious need of man is to be saved and transformed in this way by faith, when faith is not merely a belief but a giving of oneself quite completely to what has such character and power that it will transform him into the best that human life can ever reach, and save him from the worst, provided that he meets the required conditions.

Always the last phrase in the previous sentence must be added, namely, provided that he meets the required conditions. Man cannot be sustained, saved and transformed unless he decides for this and not for that, and this decision must take the form of whole-hearted self-giving, to be transformed in any way that this commitment may bring forth. There is a creativity which produces fruit and flower when required conditions are present, but will not do so when the required conditions are absent. So also there is a creativity which creates man and sustains, saves and transforms him into the best that he can become. But the difference between man on the one hand, and fruit and flower on the other, is that man must himself provide some of the required conditions, chief of which is faith. But faith is not mere intellectual assent to a proposition; it is not mere belief. All too frequently Protestants have seemed to identify faith with belief merely. Faith is precisely the kind of self-giving above noted; it is the placing of the total existing self into the power and keeping of what can shape man to his highest destiny. Faith in this sense of most complete self-giving is implied in the following words of John Calvin: "We are not our own; therefore let us not propose it as our need to seek what may be expedient for us according to the flesh. We are not our own; therefore let us, as far as possible, forget ourselves and all the things that are ours. On the contrary, we are God's; to him therefore let us live and die."

This deepest and universal need of man to commit himself in faith to what creates, sustains, saves and transforms him into the best that he can become, arises, I have said, out of the nature of man, namely, his capacity to be transformed beyond any known limit to the utmost extremes of good and evil. This need can never be satisfied unless the commitment is to something that is extra-human. It cannot be extra-human in the sense of being outside of human life. Obviously nothing can transform man unless it works in him and upon him in some way or other. In that sense it must be in human life. But it must be extra-human in the sense that it transforms man in ways other than those transformations accomplished by his own plans, purposes and ideals. This is necessary because it is precisely these plans, purposes and ideals that must be transformed along with the organization of personality. When these plans, purposes and ideals are evil, they cannot be the means of transforming man into what is good. Even when they are the best possible for the individual at his stage of development, they become wrong when made the chief means of transformation because at their best they are only transitional to something better.

Only the arrogantly and stupidly self-complacent will think that his plans, purposes and ideals are the best possible in the sense of being arrows pointing straight on to something better instead of being deviants pointing at various angles away from the line of higher transformation.

This arrogant and stupid self-complacency is one of the three human propensities which prevent men from committing themselves in faith to what can in truth transform them into the best that can be, and save them from the worst. A second propensity that prevents men from making this commitment is fear and anxiety. Man is afraid to commit himself to what will transform him in ways that he cannot foresee, even when he knows the transformation will be into something better. This fear becomes acute when it is seen that this commitment involves suffering and deprivation even though, when quite complete, it also yields peace and blessedness. The third obstacle to this commitment of faith is ignorance of what it is to which he must commit himself to be sustained, saved and transformed.

Man must have something against which to criticize and correct his highest ideals. Obviously this cannot be a higher ideal for such a claim would be a contradiction, since it is his highest ideal that is to be criticized and corrected. Therefore something else than an ideal is required. But the only alternative to an ideal is an actuality. Some actuality, then, must be that against which ideals are criticized. But no actuality can serve this purpose unless it is of greater value than any ideal, and is recognized to be such by the individual concerned. Furthermore, the individual must commit himself to it in faith after the manner above described, for otherwise he will not be able to relinquish or criticize his highest ideals and most cherished desires.

This actuality commanding religious commitment, enabling a man to correct his ideals, must be accessible to intellectual inquiry by those methods which enable a man to discover his errors. There are many alleged kinds of intellectual inquiry in the field of religion which merely serve to give divine sanction (so called) to the beliefs which one happens to hold whether these beliefs be derived from tradition or fancy. Much alleged religious inquiry turns out to be nothing more than a rationalization by which mistaken ideas and misdirected ideals are more deeply entrenched against criticism and correction. It would seem that the only reliable method for correcting preconceived ideas and rationalizations is the method that tests a proposition by observing directly or indirectly those events which must occur if the proposition is true and by the negative test of not discovering those events which must occur if the proposition is false; also by finding that the given proposition is consistent with a system of other propositions that have been confirmed by like observations. There is of course no way to render the human mind infallible. Neither this method nor any other will save from error. But there is no other method which seems better able to discover the errors that have been made than this, and no other method so well fitted to discover what is true.

Thus we reach the conclusion: What commands religious commitment of faith and thereby meets the deepest universal religious need of man must be an actuality (not an ideal) which creates, sustains, saves and transforms man into the best he can become when required conditions are present, chief of these conditions being that man commit himself to it in religious faith. Furthermore, this actuality must be accessible to empirical inquiry when empirical inquiry is understood to be the method described in the previous paragraph.

This actuality has often commanded the religious commitment of men even when they never discovered it by any kind of empirical method. This could occur in much the same way that men have often eaten wholesome food without any scientific knowledge of what wholesome food is. But these less reliable methods of guiding religious commitment of faith can no longer suffice to meet our need. Religious commitment of faith must today be guided, in part at least, by knowledge derived from the sciences, especially the social sciences. At this point many a reader will turn away in disgust. He will say that this is the claim of two generations ago and has been demonstrated to be mistaken. If the reader is of this mind I must regretfully bid him farewell. But this is the revolutionary religious transformation in doctrine and practice of religion which our age must accomplish if modern man is to be saved from self-destruction. The promise of Protestantism, as yet unfulfilled, is to meet this need and opportunity.

Religious self-criticism and religious inquiry must be more intensive. They must be stepped up by inducing more people to engage in this criticism and inquiry, especially more of the highly gifted; and more of our resources, economic and cultural, must be devoted to this criticism of religion and inquiry for religion. Furthermore, the inquiry must be based upon empirical data and the findings of the social sciences.

II

What Must Be Done

The development of Western society has reached that point which other societies in their time also reached, where the traditional forms of self-commitment no longer direct the self-giving of man to what in truth does save and transform, sustain and create into the better life. The history of civilizations seems to indicate that they all reached this point relative to the traditional religion of that time and place. When complexity, power and wealth are increased beyond a certain limit relative to the social structure, with control concentrated in the hands of a ruling minority, there is a religious task to be done. To date it seems this task never was done with sufficient thoroughness and in time to save the civilization in question. The task calls for intensive criticism of the established forms of religion combined with intensive religious inquiry, and followed by revolutionary transformation of religion to fit it to the needs of men living under the social conditions of that time. Prior to this age of magnified complexity, wealth and power with control concentrated in a ruling group, religious commitment could be correctly guided by non-cognitive myths and symbols, as, for example, the practitioner may call electricity "juice" and think of it as a flowing liquid. Thus, while the layman will always use myths and other non-cognitive symbols, whether in science or religion, there comes a time when complexity and power reach such magnitude that man will destroy himself if genuine knowledge in these areas is not to be had by men specially trained to master it. The layman can get along very well with non-cognitive symbols to guide his behaviour if some have the knowledge to keep the popular symbolism in the right channels. This is just as true in religion as it is in science. In science we do have such knowledge accessible to those specially trained. In religion we do not. Therein lies our danger. The threat that hangs over us comes not from the high development of science. It comes from the lack of development in religion.

The problem is *not* to "make religion intellectually respectable", as though the task were to make it popular and appealing to the highly trained intellect. This concern to make religion intellectually respectable is a symptom of decay in religious thought and feeling. It is not respectability, it is truth that is needed, no matter how lacking in respectability this truth may be. The religious conservatives are right in denouncing these efforts to make religion intellectually respectable, although they are wrong in refusing to undertake intensive self-criticism and intensive religious inquiry.

To show why religion must undergo this revolutionary transformation from universal use of symbols that are less accurately cognitive, over to the use of signs by the specially trained that are more accurately cognitive, I make the following analysis of our present social situation.

In making this analysis I draw upon the social sciences, especially the psychology of personality as set forth by Harry Stack Sullivan and the neo-Freudians, also anthropologists, historians and archaeologists.

Man lives at two levels. One of these might be called the top level in the sense that it dominates the personality in most complex societies; but "top" is not intended to suggest any necessary moral superiority. Each of these two levels of organization (or disorganization) in the individual is fostered and developed respectively by two kinds of interchange that go on between the individual and his associates. The one kind of interchange occurs in the form of obeying impersonal rules and regulations and responding to signals like traffic lights. All impersonal instruction is of this sort. A great part of learning in schools and elsewhere is of this kind. As society becomes more complex and as individuals exercise more power as, for example, operating a high powered automobile, there must be more of this kind of interchange between each individual and his associates. Thereby is developed what is here called the top level in the organization or disorganization of the individual personality. It is that level in which attention is highly focussed on specific things to be done and action is more or less precisely directed to doing these things. A simple illustration of this is the way individuals driving high powered cars in heavy traffic react to one another. There is no recognition, understanding and appreciation of the individual person. The traffic society is an authoritarian society in the sense that it is governed by impersonal rules and regulations and enforced by a ruling group called the police who are instructed to shoot you if you do not obey them. As a rule, no provision is made for the peculiar needs of the individual. If the peculiar needs of the individual are such that he cannot operate a car according to the rules, he is not allowed to drive a car.

This case of the traffic society is taken merely to illustrate the kind of social order that runs all through a society and tends to become increasingly dominant as wealth, power and complexity increase. This kind of social order comes to dominate the industrial plant, the merchandizing mart, government, school, church, neighborhood and even the home. This is not the only kind of interchange that occurs in a society, as we shall see. But it tends to become increasingly dominant in any society when power, wealth and complexity increase. Also it carries with it the necessity of placing the management and enforcement of this regulative system in the hands of a ruling minority. Otherwise the whole system would break down. Hence we have what has been called with some exaggeration "the managerial revolution". Top management in big industry and big labor unions acquire enormous power. So also does top management in government, both local and federal; so also does top management in the school system, in the city and elsewhere.

This kind of social order is authoritarian in the sense that it consists of a hierarchy of domination and subordination without recognition, understanding and appreciation of the individual personality. He becomes a cog in the big machine. A given individual may in one situation be at a low level in this hierarchy, as when he drives his car from home to office under the domination of impersonal rules enforced by the police, but as soon as he gets into his office he may be at a very high level if he is the chief executive in a huge corporation or the president of the United States or chief of the Federal Bureau of Investigation. While some individuals may thus pass back and forth between high and low levels in the hierarchy, while others never rise above a low level, nevertheless all are under the control of this system of impersonal subordination and domination.

What I have called the top level in the organization of personality in each individual is developed to meet the demands of this kind of social order. Persons most successful in such an order, in the sense of rising to top levels of control, are likely to be most exclusively dominated by the kind of personality-organization best fitted to meet the demands of this kind of social order. Also those most completely enslaved at the lower levels are likely to be moulded helplessly to meet these demands. Indeed every member of such a society will be shaped from early childhood at one level of its personality to meet the demands of this authoritarian impersonal system.

Over against the kind of social order just described is another kind. Human beings in every society have another way of communicating with one another besides this of responding to signals, commands, impersonal rules and regulations, abstract instruction and one way propaganda. There is another way by which they regulate their behavior toward one another besides this of subordination and domination. There is another kind of social control that can be called mutual control as over against the authoritarian. This other kind of social order and social control and social interchange can be called that of creative communication. It is the kind of communication by which I learn what you know and feel what you feel, and you learn what I know and feel what I feel.

The kind of interchange called creative communication—to distinguish this kind from what is not creative but merely regulative—is what develops all the potentialities of man that are distinctively human. What distinguishes man as distinctively human is his capacity: 1) to expand beyond any known limit what he can know, predict and control by learning from others and thus accumulating the shared findings of all men, the chief example of this being science; 2) to expand beyond any known limit what he can feel in vividness and variety of felt qualities derived from happenings and possibilities which others have experienced, the technical form of this kind of communication being art; 3) to expand beyond any known limit the sympathetic understanding of one another, widening and deepening community between each and all, the traditional name for this being Christian love; 4) to expand beyond any known limit the compass of each mind and personality by increasing the scope of what each can know, feel and love by using linguistic and other signs in creative communication, and so increasing the meaning of these signs in the three dimensions just mentioned, namely, in knowledge, feeling and love.

Now we are ready to examine again the basic religious need and the basic religious question: What is that actuality, not an ideal, operative in the midst of human life, but extra-human in the sense that it goes on all the time more or less to create, sustain, save and transform the human mind and personality, as metabolism does for the body, even when men know nothing about it and do nothing by intent to promote it and often do very much to hinder it? What is that actuality, accessible to empirical inquiry, to which man must commit himself in the total existential being of his individuality, to be sustained, saved and transformed into the best that man can ever become, and which he must serve above all else by striving in all times and at any cost to provide the conditions, physical, social and personal, which it demands in order to operate most effectively in human life? If the above analysis is correct the answer to that question is not far to seek. It is: creative communication.

This actuality going on in human life can, of course, be given many different names. It can be called the power of God unto salvation revealed in Jesus Christ, for I claim it was precisely this that was revealed in mighty power in the fellowship of Jesus and in the fellowship of his disciples after his death. It was this, I claim, that converted Saul of Tarsus into Paul

[175]

the Disciple. It was this that converted Augustine, the ambitious young lawyer into St. Augustine. It is this that operates in a church when preaching and religious symbolism are truly effective in changing the lives of men.

This actuality can be given many other names and has been given many others. The symbols and myths of the great religions at their best have directed the self-giving commitment of men to this and it is this that has produced the great saints of history, when mutual trust took the place of mutual protection against one another, when mutual control took the place of authoritarian control, when mutual love and understanding and fellowship took the place of mutual fear, hate, envy or cold and indifferent mutual adjustment.

This actuality can be called the Holy Spirit left behind, so to speak, after the death of Jesus to maintain creative communication dominant over the authoritarian order in the fellowship of those called his disciples. It can be called the living Christ that rose from the dead not in the form of a physiological organism, necessarily, but in the form of this creative communication or Christian love lifted to dominance over all else in the lives of those who rightly bore the name of Christian.

One of the discouraging features of present day religious discussion, thought and practice is the inability of sincere and devoted religious people and religious inquirers to use the same language. There is a religious language that cannot well be discarded, however great the need to define its referents more precisely. If a person insists that certain words cannot be used because irrelevant meanings inevitably stick to them, it is futile to argue with him; but such a person should be subjected to the kind of psychological treatment advocated by Count Korzybski and his followers as a cure for the ills, psychological and social, arising out of the inability to use words freely. (See *Science and Sanity* by Alfred Korzybski, also books by S. I. Hayakawa, *Language in Action,* and others who have popularized Korzybski's teachings.)

May we turn to an examination of the present state of Western society and its basic religious need. Its need is to recognize the supreme importance to man of this actuality in the midst of human life here called creative communication; to search out by all the resources of inquiry at our command the conditions that it requires in order to operate most effectively; to utilize all the power of our technology to set up and maintain these conditions so far as possible; but first and above all to lead people to commit themselves without reservation, at any cost, to this actuality to be sustained, saved and transformed progressively into the fullest realization of the potentialities of human life.

The statement just made is not intended to suggest that no further religious inquiry is needed to gain a better knowledge of what has such extra-human character and power that man must by faith commit himself to it. What I have said is intended only to suggest the direction which religious inquiry might take. One cannot conduct any kind of inquiry by running off in all directions and trying to search out the nature of everything indiscriminately. Inquiry must be focused and the area defined. This only I have tried to do.

There is a vicious process that operates in the authoritarian order of society as complexity, wealth and power increase. In time this brings irreparable disaster, destruction and the doom of that civilization if it is not countered. It cannot be countered except by religious self-criticism, religious inquiry and religious revolution leading to more accurate religious knowledge and intelligent religious practice by which men are led to commit themselves as above noted. Also in this way only can they be led to use their wealth and power to set up and maintain the conditions demanded by the power of God in their midst, here interpreted to be Christian love or creative communication.

This vicious process can be described after the following manner. As the order of impersonal domination and subordination increases, those individuals who find all their satisfaction in dominating others and who are thereby peculiarly addicted to and fitted for dominating, rise to places of supreme control. Being what they are, they magnify the authoritarian order throughout society and suppress the order of creative communication. This moulds each person from early childhood so that the dominant organization of his personality is fitted to meet the demands of this order, while his capacity for creative communication is suppressed or never developed. But the need for creative communication, the need to be recognized, appreciated, understood, loved, never, it seems, dies in the human being. (See *Interpersonal Relations* edited by Patrick Mullahy; *Child and Society* by Erik Erikson; books by Erich Fromm, especially *The Forgotten Language,* books by Karen Horney, especially *Neurosis and Human Growth.*)

When this need is not satisfied, and the cry to be appreciated, understood and loved is stifled and driven into the unconscious, the members of such a society become increasingly restive and discontented. They begin to hate themselves in the sense that one part of the self opposes the other part. The authoritarian organization of personality beats down that other part of the personality which cries for creative communication; while this part that seeks to love and be loved, to appreciate and be appreciated, constantly threatens to throw off the domination of the authoritarian self. All this generates hate. It also generates hate, fear and envy toward others. These hates and fears are concealed from self consciousness by devices widely recognized in the psychology of personality. Thus hate, fear, suspicion, envy, rebellion against oneself and others increase throughout the social order. In the meantime, persons more and more driven by the lust to dominate rise to places of supreme control and intensify the order of domination and subordination to the exclusion of creative communication. Furthermore, the places of supreme control are limited in number and many who have this lust and the ability to exercise this kind of social control, cannot attain the high positions. So there is struggle for power that becomes more intense, until the society must either go to war against some other society to give outlet for the persons who cannot exercise such domination in time of peace, or else there must be internal struggles mounting in time to rebellion, revolution and civil strife. All the time the creative potentialities of that society are being reduced.

Obviously such a process cannot go on indefinitely. To be sure many conditions may develop that counteract it without regard to any intelligent action directed by men to that end. But in time this vicious process will drag down to ruin the civilization that harbors it unless the kind of religious transformation occurs that has been described. To date every civilization has been dragged down by this vicious internal process.

Western society has reached the turning point where this destructive process must be countered else there is no hope for us. This is the religious need and the religious opportunity of our time. To this task Protestantism has been called. To this end it was brought forth some 400 years ago. Whether or not it will measure up to the opportunity and the need remains to be seen. But it has certain capacities which might be lifted from the level of latency to the level of full exercise and if this were done it might show the way of salvation both for the individual and for our society. Let us then examine the structure and content of Protestantism with this in mind.

III

Can Protestantism Meet the Need?

Justification by faith alone lies at the heart of Protestantism. Whatever else this doctrine means, it affirms that the individual has direct relation to God, intimate, personal and destiny-determining. It affirms that no set of doctrines can be a substitute for this direct personal encounter; no sacraments, no official ministration of the church, no institutional structure or office of the church, can be allowed to intervene. All these are secondary, instrumental and subject to correction and improvement according as they do or do not enable the individual to have this meeting with God.

Obviously this approach opens the way for endless inquiry, profound criticism and correction of doctrine, practice and the structure of the church. It reveals the capacity of Protestantism to meet the need of our time as that need has been analyzed and described.

It is further the teaching of Protestantism that the individual cannot discern the presence of God in the divine encounter unless God himself takes the initiative in awakening this apprehension of the holy presence. This awakened awareness of God combined with repentance for sin and the self-giving of religious commitment are unitedly called faith.

Faith understood to be as stated is impossible apart from the recognition that one is in the state of sin. Recognizing sin in oneself and recognizing the reality of God are inseparable because they are obverse sides of the same thing. This becomes obvious when one sees how the human mind comes to know anything whatsoever. To know what anything is, one must be able to distinguish it from what it is not, especially must one distinguish it from its contradictory opposite. God and sin are contradictory opposites. Sin is that directon of the will, *i.e.,* that organization of personality, that is opposed to God. Therefore blindness to sin blinds one to God. To discern God is also to discern what is opposed to God in oneself. Therefore recognition of one's own sin and repentance are a necessary part of that awakened awareness toward God and that self-giving to God which make up what is called faith.

Since faith is the giving of oneself over to God to serve him above all and to be transformed by his creative, sustaining and saving power into what God alone can make of men, obviously this involves the repudiation of everything in oneself that runs counter to the demands and ways of God. The name given to everything in oneself that runs counter to the demands and ways of God is sin. Therefore the repudiation of sin, otherwise called repentance, is necessarily involved in any genuine turning toward God. How anyone can deny this I do not understand. However, I do understand the disgust that many people feel for the maudlin and morbid talk about sin, and the ridiculous or monstrous misinterpretation of what sin is. All this explains the aversion which many people have toward the whole idea of sin. The word may become unusable, like the word "God" and many other ancient terms, but the ancient realities are there just the same and they are inescapable determinants of human destiny.

The repudiation of sin called repentance does not, of course, render one sinless. But by this repudiation one looks upon his sin as alien to himself in so far as he is committed to God. He repudiates his sin in order to be allied with God. The only other alternative, since the two are diametrically opposed to one another, is to repudiate God in order to be allied with sin.

The forgiveness of sin is not different and not separable from the divine initiative which awakens in a man the awareness of God, the sense of sin, repentance and the self-giving of faith. Furthermore when we examine the actual historical cases where all this has occurred, namely, awakened awareness, conviction of sin, repentance and the self-giving of faith, all of which adds up to the forgiveness of sin, we find that the divine initiative always assumes the form of creative communication lifted to dominance in some other life or fellowship and acting upon the individual with power to transform him. Such was the case of Paul and Augustine. Such is the case of all the recorded instances. The culminating moment when one is conscious of undergoing the transformation may be when he is alone reading some scrap of scripture or traveling on the road to Damascus or lying on the stairs of the Cathedral in Rome or wherever. But a study of the case always reveals in the background the power of creative communication with some individual or group.

But all these matters just described in Protestantism have what I call a ragged edge. There is an incompleteness, an indefiniteness, a vagueness, a lack of the criteria of truth which cannot continue if Protestantism is to survive. How does one know that it is God to which one has been awakened, meaning, how does one know that it is what has such extra-human character and power that man must commit himself to it to be sustained, saved and transformed? How does one know that it is sin which one is repudiating and not the very righteousness demanded by the real deity? Observation of many cases will reveal that this horrible error has been perpetrated and the whole apparatus of religion has become a device for sanctifying the arrogance, cruelty and error of man. Observation reveals this in the sense that what one individual has called God and sin are the diametrical opposites to what others have so named. Therefore if the one is correct, the other is not.

The answer given by many Protestants to this question: 'How do you know that what you call God and sin are truly so?' is simply to say: Jesus Christ. God is revealed in Jesus Christ and in Christ we know what is God and what is opposed to God.

This may sound very conclusive and definite when spoken by a faithful Catholic because the Catholic church provides explicit and detailed directions and interpretations of what is to be understood as the revelation of God in Christ. But Protestantism has rejected all that and throws the individual back upon his own resources after the manner above described. To be sure the Protestant has the entire Christian tradition to guide him, he has the fellowship of believers, he has the Bible, he has all the teachings of the church and in addition all the teachings of the other great religions of the world, not to mention the wisdom and literature of the ages to cover everything not listed otherwise. But how can the individual make use of all this? The Catholic has a definite body of doctrine and practice to guide him. So does the Protestant, one may reply. Yes, but the essential nature of Protestantism removes from this guiding body of doctrine and practice that definiteness and finality which it has for the Catholic. As previously explained, according to Protestantism, the individual stands face to face with God and all these teachings and practices from whatsoever source are but ways and means for communing with God or otherwise dealing with the ultimate reality of the divine. Hence they all are subject to reinterpretation, criticism, correction or discarding, according as the demands of this divine encounter may require.

Now so long as a single coherent and unifying tradition served to guide the commitment of faith this indefiniteness, this lack of criteria to distinguish the true from the false, the divine from the demonic, did not expose the individual to chaos and the dark as he groped for the divine reality. But there is no such coherent and unifying tradition today or rather it is decaying and disintegrating before our eyes and all the desperate attempts to reestablish it are in vain. Indeed, this is precisely what has always happened in every civilization relative to its traditional religion when it reached a high level of complexity, power and wealth. Always, the attempt to restore the ancient ways and the old tradition has failed and it always will. It will today. Some other guide must be found. Some other criteria must be established for distinguishing between the divine and the demonic when a man stands before the abyss of all being with nothing to show him the way. In such a situation a man may follow Sartre and the atheistic existentialists, or Kierkegaard and the theistic existentialists such as Tillich, Barth and the Niebuhr brothers who repudiate the possibility of any intellectual guidance concerning these ultimate issues.

But Protestantism cannot survive without better guidance in this matter of ultimate religious commitment. For more important than the survival of Protestantism, modern man cannot find the way of salvation without better intellectual guidance than Protestantism is now able to provide. The one asset Protestantism has is its capacity to undergo intensive self-criticism, to conduct intensive religious inquiry and to undergo the revolutionary transformation enabling it to provide the

[183]

kind of guidance that modern man must have to find the way from death unto a way of living wherein knowledge and power can expand indefinitely, wherein richness of felt quality can increase and where breadth and depth of sympathetic understanding between individuals and groups can grow with the flowering of the human mind and personality in community. Thus Protestantism is under coercion either to exercise its threefold capacity or else gradually sink into futility.

The consequences of this vagueness and indefiniteness of Protestantism on these ultimate issues is revealed in the ever shifting and hopeless dialectic between theonomy, heteronomy and autonomy, set forth by Paul Tillich, Wilhelm Pauck and James Adams. Within the framework of their religious beliefs this endless shift from one to the other of these three alternates is inevitable. But the hopeless futility of such inevitable misdirection of life becomes unendurable. There is another and better way attainable if more reliable criteria can be found for guiding the theonomous way of life. If these more reliable criteria are not found by intensive inquiry and revolutionary transformation, the religious need and opportunity of our time will pass unmet and our society will move on to its doom. Some religious leaders seem not much disturbed by this doom since it may turn men back to the traditional formulations of the faith and thus enhance the power and prestige of the religious leaders who champion these formulations. It may well be that they will have their reward.

One further characteristic of Protestantism must be mentioned because it reveals its threefold capacity to meet the religious need of our time and also the dangerous lack of criteria for distinguishing truth and error. The freedom of the Christian man as set forth by Luther and by many another Protestant reveals this capacity and this danger. The Christian man under Protestantism is free to find God for himself and to live under the supreme control of God, thus delivered from the ultimacy of every other control. Of course the Christian man will obey the laws of the state and adapt himself to all the other requirements of social living. But for him none of these are ultimate. Therefore under God he can criticize, oppose, reject any of them if the will of God in him should so demand. Here I stand, so help me God. I cannot do otherwise, even though all the powers of church and state be against me.

Having found existentially in his own life the actual events that are the living God, he is free to seek for more truth about God beyond the doctrines of his church and his society. He is free to criticize doctrines, practices, institutions and offices now prevailing, for all these are imperfect interpretations and instrumentalities for understanding, serving and living in the power and keeping of those events which are the actual God. The individual who has found God in this way can confidently stand against the world, including opposition to the entire body of religious thought and practice. He may be mistaken in his criticism, rejections, proposals and substitutions, but he is right in the claim that the living God is very different from all of these and much more than all of these, just as every concrete event is always very different from, and much more than, all that can be said and done about it.

Such is the freedom of the Christian man under Protestantism. But obviously this puts a tremendous burden on the criteria by which one distinguishes the divine from the demonic. Hitler might conceivably have thought of himself as free under God after this fashion. Certainly many a fanatic and many who are put into insane asylums think and feel after this fashion. The claim that one has this freedom only when he confronts Jesus Christ in the Bible and thereby finds God is very much too vague and indefinite. In the name of Christ, old women have been burned as witches, the cruelest of wars have been fought, hundreds have been tortured. In the name of Christ, Negroes are lynched, White Supremacy proclaimed and in Christian Science the reality of matter denied. Confronting Christ by way of the Bible obviously is no reliable guide for the conduct of human living.

I have suggested that there is an actuality going on in human life that can be searched by the resources of all the sciences to understand better what it demands of us and what conditions, physical, personal and social, are required for it to dominate our lives and bring to its servitude the authoritarian social order that is now increasingly dominant over everything else. I have called it creative communication and it is a process that can be studied like any other. I claim, furthermore, that this is precisely what was revealed in Jesus Christ and his fellowship, because the conditions, psychological, social, historical, were then present so that these, when combined with the kind of person that Jesus was, enabled creative communication (or Christian love) to rise to dominance in the lives of these men. It continued to dominate in the fellowship that went on after his death. It is the power of God unto salvation for the individual and for society, when it rises to dominance over the authoritarian order and over all other impulses and habits of the individual. It does thus rise to dominance when men commit themselves to it and provide the other required conditions as these are discovered by the social sciences.

If I am wrong in pointing to creative communication (or Christian love) as having that extra-human character and power which alone can sustain, save and transform, then my error must be made known by demonstrating something else to have this character and this power. I am mainly concerned not that this particular interpretation be accepted, although I shall defend it until my error is brought home to me; but I am mainly concerned that all the resources of religious self-criticism and inquiry be mobilized to find and establish better criteria than we now have to guide the commitment of faith.

As bees make honey, as eagles soar and flowers bloom, so man is made for creative communication. This is the entelechy of men. The creativity that works in the world has at last broken free in the life of man to create the mind distinctively human, to expand it beyond any known limit in community, with widening horizons of knowledge, power and love and with beauty in the form of vivid and varied felt qualities experienced in the happenings and possibilities of the world. The ancient prophets have called this work of God in the life of man the Kingdom of God. To place this Kingdom in another world, meaning beyond history, is to betray the great prophets who proclaimed a Kingdom of God attainable in the temporal world.

The release of creativity in the life of man to bring forth this fulfillment waits on a form of faith that can guide man's commitment and man's service more wisely than any form of religion that has yet existed. No institutional structure of religious doctrine and practice has yet attained a form competent to carry man over that peak of complexity, wealth and power which high civilization produces. To achieve this form of faith is the promise of Protestantism. This is the *whither* of that promise. Whether this promise will be fulfilled is not yet known. The whither and the whether of Protestantism will be determined in the years to come.

SUGGESTIONS FOR FURTHER READING

ARTHUR CUSHMAN MCGIFFERT, *Christianity Since the Reformation.*
HAROLD BOSLEY, *The Church Militant* (New York, 1952).
WILHELM PAUCK, *The Heritage of the Reformation* (Boston, 1950).
DANIEL DAY WILLIAMS, *God's Grace and Man's Hope* (New York, 1949).
REINHOLD NIEBUHR, *The Nature and Destiny of Man* (New York, 1946).
STRINGFELLOW BARR, *The Pilgrimage of Western Man* (New York, 1949).
PAUL TILLICH, *The Protestant Era* (Chicago, 1948).
———, *Systematic Theology,* Vol. I (Chicago, 1951).
WINFRED ERNEST GARRISON, *A Protestant Manifesto* (Nashville, 1952).
JAMES NICHOLS, *Primer for Protestants* (New York, 1947).
GREGORY VLASTOS, *The Religious Way* (New York, 1934).
BERNARD MELAND, *The Seeds of Redemption* (New York, 1947).

CAN PROTESTANTISM COME OF AGE?

By

FLOYD H. ROSS

Floyd H. Ross

*A new star appeared on the firmament of religious author-
ship in the publication in 1950 of a little book called "Addressed to Christians". Its author is Dr. Floyd Ross who, for
more than a decade, has been associated with the faculty of
the School of Religion in the University of Southern California.
He is a professor of World Religions. Born in Indianapolis,
Indiana, he was graduated from Butler University in 1930,
with a B.D. from Garrett Seminary in 1933, an M.A. from
Northwestern University in 1933 and a Ph.D. from Yale in
1935. He began his teaching career at Iowa Wesleyan College
in Iowa and taught one year at Southern Methodist University
in its department of religion. For many years he held membership in the Methodist church. He now holds his church affilia-
tion with the Wider Quaker Fellowship and also with the
Neighborhood Church (Congregational) of Pasadena. "Addressed to Christians" is a daring and prophetic book calling
for the Christians in the churches to take a fresh look at things.
A world community calls for an appropriate theology framed
in hypotheses and premises very different from those in the
tradition. Christians must look toward a world parliament of
religions, even transcending the sectarianism of Protestantism
itself. Other of his publications are: "Personalism and the
Problem of Evil" (1940); "Ethics and the Modern World"
(co-authorship, 1952); "The Meaning of Life in Hinduism
and Buddhism" (1952); and "The Crisis in Western Faith"
(co-authorship, 1952). The catholicity of his outlook goes beyond ecumenicity as presently conceived by Protestants. Thus,
here is one of the new voices calling for a grand reorientation
of thought within the Protestant household.*

Editor

CAN PROTESTANTISM COME OF AGE?

FLOYD H. ROSS

Your daily life is your temple and your religion.
Whenever you enter into it take with you your all.
Take the plough and the forge and the mallet and the lute,
The things you have fashioned in necessity or for delight. . .
And take with you all men.

Kahlil Gibran, The Prophet

IF PROTESTANTISM is to be identified with its prevailing beliefs and practices, then I would have to admit that I am not a Protestant. I find it impossible to separate religion from life, or the temple from the market-place, or the Christian from the non-Christian. In the twentieth century it is not only absurd but dangerous to ask people to swear a loyalty oath to any segment of the human past if it means potentially excluding from the fellowship of seekers those who cannot accept my labels, formulas, or beliefs. A modern Jew, David Daiches, has well said that "the jealous guarding of the integrity of a religious or cultural tradition was justified only in ages when each cultural or religious group was guarding some special aspect of the truth which was denied or ignored by other groups".

That time is past, in my estimation.

If Protestantism is broad enough and deep enough to include in its fellowship all honest seekers—a Ramakrishna and a Gandhi along with a Jacob Boehme and a William Penn, Gautama Buddha along with Roger Williams, Socrates along with Francis of Assisi—any one of us can be glad to join such a company of pilgrims. It took Martin Luther years to see many of the implications of his initial act in raising some fundamental questions regarding the Roman Catholic practice of selling indulgences. Even by the time he died, Luther was not aware of some of the profounder implications of his break with an authoritarian system. It is up to contemporary Protestants to carry that radical inquiry much farther if modern Western man is to escape both the authoritarianism of the "Right" and the authoritarianism of the "Left". At least two basic questions are involved in this reexamination: 1) the relationship between Christianity and the non-Christian traditions of the world; 2) the profounder implications of modern psychological concepts as related to the dynamics of the growth process (in more traditional terms, the problem of reconciliation and redemption). In the first case, Christians must look again at their most treasured symbols and convictions regarding the centrality of the Hebrew-Christian revelation and the "Lordship of Jesus." In the second case, closer attention must be given to the psychological insights made possible by the study of the dynamics of interpersonal relationships whether in terms of Freudian, Jungian, or other suggestive hypotheses.

*   *   *   *   *   *

Most tribal groupings of human beings on this planet at one time or another seem to have regarded themselves as "divinely chosen" for special privileges or special responsibilities. Sooner or later these tribal conceits or prejudices have usually been transcended or outgrown, with a few outstanding exceptions such as the Hebrews and the Christians. In the case of both these religions, the conviction of chosenness has been held with tenacity down through the centuries. A person either shares such a conviction or he does not; there is no "in between" position. The conviction is either true or untrue—but there is no conceivable way in which its truth or falsity can be established. Those who insist that Christianity must be interpreted as involving the idea of chosenness and "special revelation" cannot understand those who insist that such an interpretation is not necessary, and *vice versa.* Those who claim that Christianity alone has the divine promise or the only savior of mankind are uttering a dogma which is no more self-evident to a non-Christian than the Roman Catholic dogma of the primacy of Peter is self-evident to a Protestant.

A. K. Coomaraswamy has said, "We cannot establish human relationships with other peoples if we are convinced of our own superiority or superior wisdom, and only want to convert them to our way of thinking. The modern Christian, who thinks of the world as his parish, is faced with the painful necessity of becoming himself a citizen of the world." One of the favorite missionary hymns concludes with the verse,

> Can we, whose souls are lighted
> With wisdom from on high,
> Can we to men benighted
> The lamp of life deny?

Is this one of the inevitable by-products of asserting that one belongs to the "true Israel", "the chosen of God"? Is this just a sophisticated way of saying that there is *a restrictive covenant in God's grace?* What lies back of the inability to see the fruits of the life of the spirit under other labels, "names" and forms?

Perhaps in the next fifty years Protestants will seriously grapple with this whole problem. The need is for many a Clement and Origen, a John Scotus Eriugena and a John Hus, a modern Thomas Aquinas and a Martin Luther; plus the need for many others who will refuse to regard such modern pioneers as having said the last word. Too often have churches been schools for timidity and narrowness of spirit. "Slavery to tradition, fear of inquiry, submission to institutions are not religion but the want of it, not faith but unbelief." (John Oman, *Honest Religion*.) When Protestantism has broadened its base and deepened its perspective on this problem, it will have shown its capacity for transcending the confining forms of the past.

In reassessing basic Christian assumptions, such as that of

special chosenness, Protestants will be forced to dig down into the deeper areas of the human mind. Why does indoctrination always tend to displace education? Why are so-called religious folk, earnest Christians even, bedevilled so much by anxiety about the morrow and the after-life? Why is it that the testimony of the lives of rank and file Christians is as confusing and indecisive as the testimony of the lives of unbelievers? The modern depth psychologies, along with the penetrating insights of the ancient Upanishadic sages and Gautama Buddha, may throw a great deal of light on such questions. The problem of *anxiety* (which Gautama called the problem of *duhkha*—dis-ease) may well prove to be the decisive problem. Certainly the evidence is accumulating that Augustine, the bishop of Hippo, did not give a definite solution to the problem of man's nature or predicament even though he was the first profound psychologist the Western church produced.

Man's anxious search for security-at-almost-any-price is revealed, among other ways, in his tendencies to sell out to fixed dogmas, an arbitrary priesthood, or an authoritarian non-personal system. Every religious system tends to hardening of the arteries through the years. The fact that Protestantism reaffirmed the early Christian principle of freedom from the law (freedom from legalism, formalism and institutionalism) has not kept Protestants from succumbing to institutional arthritis. Too many of the Protestant churches and ministers today are still jealously guarding what they regard as some definitive revelation from the past. Religious leaders who do this seem to work on the assumption that their most radical function is to pour new wine into old wine-skins. They ignore nature's simplest lesson: each year the grape vine produces new grapes, *including new skins.*

Nature works in the human body by continuously sloughing off the old skin and tissue. To grow means to be perpetually dying to the old and to be perennially reborn to the new. This has been asserted by eminent Christians of past centuries, but exponents of such simple truths have never been received too cordially by those self-appointed "guardians of the Faith". On closer examination the "Faith" which is being guarded usually turns out to be certain institutional prerogatives as expressed in dogma, creed or rite. In other words, it is not *faith* but the pride, prejudice and insecurity-feelings of those who delight either in running an institution or in bowing down to those who do. Protestants are just as prone to cling to partial insights as non-Protestants.

Clinging—a Sign of Lack of Faithfulness

Man is a tool-using animal. However, when man is delivered over to fear and anxiety, he becomes a tool-clutching animal. The very tool which was designed to help him accomplish a fruitful result becomes a dead weight holding him back. This is very true of all fixed ideas, creeds, religious institutions. The church becomes something to *cling* to rather than something to *grow* through. As an ancient psychologist pointed out, "Anything when clung to, falls short".

The Protestant churches have fallen short again and again because they have encouraged people to cling to them. Each has often been more concerned about expressing pride over its heritage and its peculiar practices than in helping persons look at their own problems in contemporary terms. Every religious institution tends to fall short for the same set of reasons. It becomes more interested in perpetuating its own rites and rights than in helping persons develop to the place where they no longer need the institution as formerly conceived. Getting people into churches is not necessarily any more desirable or fruitful than getting people to buy Buicks or television sets. Helping people to understand how they can use churches, motor cars or television so that true spiritual growth takes place is much more important.

A child climbs a ladder by alternately seizing and letting go the rungs. When the child "fixates" on one rung and will not let go, we know that some basic fear or anxiety has seized the child. Unfortunately many people in religious institutions are like the child who has suddenly "frozen" to one rung of the ladder. It is this clinging which is the signal of lack of faith, of dis-ease or anxiety.

Each person must come to his own understanding of experience *at his own tempo*. Each infant learns to walk when it is ready. Maturing persons in a sense build the ladder by which they rise from one experience or insight to another. But he who clings to one particular experience as though it were final or definitive denies God, life, growth—no matter how valuable that particular experience may have been at that particular time in one's life history.

Nobody needs to cling to the past. The past holds each person in a friendly embrace, for the past is summed up in some sense in the chromosomes, in the cultural milieu into which one is born, in the total cosmic matrix. The universe is not over-solicitous about man: it gives of itself to each infant without demanding that the infant shall "remember" that the sun shone upon Abraham, Isaac and Jacob, or that the mountain produced water for Moses and welcome shade for a disgruntled Jonah. It is parents, priests, adults generally who are over-solicitous and who insist upon dragging in irrelevant concepts about the past. These concepts are irrelevant for the simple reason that "God is God of the living", that is, growth only takes place in the *present*.

To the extent that the adults around the child are over-concerned about family history because of their own failure to mature properly at their normal tempo, to that extent the child catches much of the same insecurity-feelings that plague the parents and the priests. He will be conditioned to accept their institutional biases and historical prejudices as though they truly reflected the life process in a profound sense. He will be taught to genuflect when they genuflect, talk theology as they talk it, verbalize the mystery of being in the same language in which they verbalize. Having done this for the first six or eight years of his life, he will find it very difficult to depart from those ways in succeeding years without strong guilt feelings or markedly neurotic symptoms.

Many Protestants are caught in this strait-jacket of their own confusion. There are ample resources in the reported sayings of Jesus and in Luther's emphasis upon "Christian liberty" and the priesthood of all believers for severing these bonds. Unfortunately most Protestants have been too much under the influence of certain aspects of the thought of Paul and of the Reformation thinkers to develop a more profound psychology of human nature. They often discuss life's profoundest problems as though Paul, Augustine and Luther "did it all". Great as these men were in spite of all their personal limitations, they should never have been regarded as definitive interpreters of the life of the spirit of man. *There is no definitive interpreter.* It is weak, faltering and immature disciples or "followers" who create the "definitive interpreter". They create him out of their own fear and trembling. They create him out of their desire for "answers", out of a compulsion for certainty and out of a desperate attempt to take out insurance against insecurity.

If a person sat down to his daily meal and went through the elaborate rigmarole that the speculative theologian goes through in trying to persuade himself that man is "justified by faith", he would die of hunger. No human being actually needs to be informed about what Paul and Luther said about redemption or reconciliation before he can experience relationships that are qualitatively redemptive. The average theologian is a nervous, verbal word-magician: unless a life process is neatly labelled, pigeonholed or cast into a paradoxical form, the life process just can't "be". Unless water is *called* water, it cannot satisfy thirst!

Since man is a self-conscious being who talks and builds concepts, each must learn how to articulate for himself as adequately as possible "the faith that is in him". But no man should take himself so seriously as to substitute his articulated system (theological or otherwise) for the mystery or reality of life and God which he will continuously explore so long as there is life in him. The theologians all too often leave the distinct impression that they are persons who can never laugh at themselves or their feeble constructions. A few more men like Socrates in the churches might save us from the error of taking ourselves so seriously.

Theologies as "Projection-Systems"

All persons have "projection-systems". That is, their interpretations of life get conceptualized or pictorialized and thus "projected" out on the world of experience as a movie-projector throws images on a screen. A child cannot think without pictures. Neither can an adult, although in many cases the adults' pictures will be more subtle. My five-year-old says to me, "Daddy, I wish you would get wings and fly up to God." (He has picked up this particular theology from his playmates, not around home.) Thomas Aquinas writes several long paragraphs regarding the angels. Both the five-year-old and Thomas are engaging in the pleasant pastime of trying to conceive the inconceivable. One of the major differences is that adult Thomases naively assume that their pictures are somehow nearer the truth-of-things than the pictures of children. A normal, healthy child in a friendly personal environment outgrows his naive picture-thinking progressively unless the adults "fixate" him on their personally preferred level of frozen concepts. Children learn to cling because parents and teachers are clinging.

All projections serve a temporary purpose. They help a growing person relate himself to processes which he does not really understand but which he must cope with somehow. Projection-systems can be refined indefinitely. A person who has prayed zealously to the saints as well as to the "Mother of God" may relinquish prayers to the saints and Mary and pray only to Jesus. This does not necessarily imply "growth in grace" or, in modern language, growth in spiritual maturity. It is possible to cling just as tenaciously to Jesus as "Lord and

Savior" as to cling to Mariolatry. It is the *clinging* which needs further analysis, not what is clung to. For it is the clinging which indicates some internal blockage, some lack of dynamic faith.

Both religions and theologies are "projection-systems". People cling to them to the extent that the life of God is not flowing freely through them. Jesus seemed to be very much aware of this, as was Gautama Buddha. It has been well said that Jesus' purpose was "to put an end to religion". Likewise with Buddha and other great teachers. Such teachers teach *persons* rather than religion. The disciples, with their tendency to lean upon a dominant personality, teach *religion* and only incidentally persons. This never pleases the ecclesiastical hierarchy of course, which likes to foster the opinion that through furthering religion it is "saving" persons. There are still persons who insist that the way to break a child of "thumb-sucking" is to put some device either on the thumb or in the roof of the child's mouth (the equivalent of religious sanctions). A profounder psychology recognizes that the child outgrows his thumb-sucking when the subtle emotional factors in his internal and interpersonal relationships have been clarified or released. In some analogous fashion people outgrow their projection-systems—unless the ecclesiastical authorities have fastened devices upon their consciousness.

Protestantism becomes just another device or "religion" when it persists in teaching that certain doctrines are indispensable to the abundant life or salvation. This is to ask people to cling to the road-signs instead of encouraging them to make their own journey with confidence. There is a Christian hymn which goes, "Make me a captive, Lord, and then I shall be free". Unfortunately, there are too many people who are altogether too sure that they *know* the "Lord", ultimate reality, the mystery of reconciliation, or redemption from fragmentary living. Too many persons are not "made captive" by the "Lord", thus finding true freedom; they are made captive by some adult's *concept* of what ultimate is or should be.

It is absurd to claim that there is any genuine freedom in being made captive by *any* concept, even though the emotional overtones associated with the concept give the false feeling of freedom.

We could learn many of these things from closer observation of children. (Have not the followers of Jesus persisted in trying to shunt the children off to one side, as the disciples did? We hate to admit that Jesus may have meant it when he said, "Of such is the kingdom of heaven".) A child explores his world with true wonder long before he understands what the adults mean by the "numinous" or the "holy" or "mysterium tremendum". He does not need to be told in solemn tones "Only God can make a tree" before discovering the God-given thrill of climbing it, feeling its rough bark against his hands and face, sensing the joy of a new experience. Out of such experiences in the life of a child comes a quickened sense of self-worth which has its important ramifications for all his relationships with other persons. The child gains a deepened sense of self and universe and God through concrete, immediate, unlabelled experiences. It is the parent who hovers, as it were, around the base of the tree with Bible in hand, wanting to label a truly religious experience "Methodist", "Baptist" or "Christian".

Too many parents are too subject to the frozen labels of adult experience, drawn from the vocabulary of the Pharisees, Sadducees and scribes who confuse life with formulas about it. Let parents learn from their children. What the growing child feels about trees, birds, bugs and snails is a vital part of what he learns to think and feel about himself, about other persons, about life, about God.

An Experimental Approach

Such terms as God, life, faith, growth are all dynamic, not static except in the hands of those who stereotype life because the life flow has stopped in their own experience. Life or God cannot be caught in a capsule, book or cathedral any more than the wind can be caught in a box. Wind in a box soon becomes stale air. Did Jesus have sound reasons for staying away from the temple precincts most of the time? Was Jesus perhaps aware that the true "church" is found simply where there is a fellowship of honest seekers or concerned persons?

The implications of this type of approach to life should be wrestled with concretely by those who call themselves Protestants. For one thing, it involves a truly experimental approach to the fundamental problems of living. No book can ever again be regarded as definitive, no teacher and no teaching. Glorying in a rich past can not be substituted for honest exploration in the living present. People who seem unable to forget that their ancestors came to America on the Mayflower are more often a stumbling-block in a dynamic society than stepping-stones.

Furthermore, no teacher or group of teachings shall be regarded as anything more than a basis for stimulating exploration, wondering, questioning. More specifically, all historic dogmas about Jesus, his "person" or rôle, shall be put as questions, not as answers. The child's experience in living can be enriched by drawing upon the questions raised by all great teachers—Zoroaster, Confucius, Gautama, Socrates, Spinoza, Krishnamurti and many others. This will help to keep the child from getting the false idea that only in the history of the Hebrews did human beings raise significant questions.

The first task of education is to strengthen the *rapport* between parents and their offspring. Where there is a true sense of *rapport* and mutual worthfulness, only good can come of adults sharing their own unanswered questions and wonderings with the oncoming generation. All teaching becomes mutual sharing and mutual exploration. Families and churches can be museums dedicated to the past, to "the dear, dead days beyond recall". Or they can be laboratories wherein fellow-pilgrims seek to raise the questions that matter most. Indoctrination is thus ruled out. A laboratory engages in fundamental research.

Protestants generally must become clearer as to the difference between education and indoctrination. The average Protestant church has many people who, in the apt phrase of Angus McLean, are spending their time being the bell-hops of history, passing on the baggage of the past to the children of the present. No one should take false consolation in the thought that the baggage passed on by Protestants is less cumbersome than that passed on by some other groups. Baggage-passing is not the highest form of education.

Education recognizes that end and means are inseparable. Method becomes of tremendous importance: *how* one teaches the child is every bit as important as *what* is taught. What happens to the child while he is "in the way" is much more important than trying to get him to come out at some parentally preconceived end. Parents have no business trying to "live out" their own unlived lives in their children. Those who try to do so are not loving their children (as they may claim to be doing) but are in love with their own ego-needs. Well intentioned but emotionally confused parents always try to live their children's lives for them. It is an important function of the church to help such parents become spiritually mature so they may learn how to guide rather than block their children's growth.

The parent or teacher who seeks to "indoctrinate" a child is not truly respecting the child's potentiality, "the image of God" in him. As the Talmud well puts it, "Limit not thy children to thine own ideas. They are born in a different time". He who indoctrinates a child is in effect shouting at the child. Such shouting springs from a form of ego-assertion or adult pride which in turn is usually rooted in insecurity feelings or frustrations. (The parent who is frustrated by a child resorts to aggressive techniques almost as often as the child, but the parent's pressure techniques are more subtle usually, less physical.) To slip over into the "shouting attitude" is evidence that one is more interested in "making a point" than in helping the child grow. He who has to insist upon making a point against a relatively immature child is saying much more about himself than about his concern for the child.

Education is concerned with "bringing out" of a person his latent potentialities (e duco, Latin—to lead out). Indoctrination is concerned with "pouring in". Education takes place in an atmosphere of permissiveness and stresses wonder, curiosity, adventuresomeness. Indoctrination takes place in an atmosphere of discipline, efficiency, conformity; it stresses the virtue of obedience. In education the participants are relaxed, at ease, confident. In indoctrination the participants tend to be brittle and anxious. Education is essentially non-coercive whereas the indoctrinator is coercive, dogmatic, definitive in approach.

An ancient Chinese writing says, "The world is a divine vessel. It cannot be shaped nor can it be insisted upon. Those who insist upon it damage it." This is borne out by careful analysis of what happens when adults become unduly coercive with children. The child can be made to conform to the adult pattern but at a tremendous price internally which poisons later relationships. Children brought up in a too authoritarian atmosphere, being forced to accept conformity against their wills, tend to demand conformity from their playmates. Characteristics such as rigidity, struggle for "status" and power, are thus aggravated. When children's feelings are violated too often, they tend to compensate by violating the feelings of others of their own age.

"Truths of life" are not something which can be conceptually imparted. They are not something to be "believed in" or legislated for others, especially children. They are to be progressively realized or assimilated in one's daily life, the realm of interpersonal relationships. The acorn is not asked to believe that it "ought" to become a fine sturdy oak because some great acorn in the past made the grade, thereby setting the example for all little acorns in the present. Nor does the acorn have a nervous breakdown trying to become a Sequoia or a pine tree. It becomes the oak through actualizing its inborn characteristics.

Beliefs, then, are quite secondary, especially verbalized beliefs. How they are gained and what they point toward are very important, however. Sophia Fahs has put this very concisely.

> Some beliefs are like pleasant gardens with high walls
>   around them.
> They encourage exclusiveness, and the feeling of being
>   especially privileged.
> Other beliefs are expansive and lead the way into wider
>   and deeper sympathies.
> Some beliefs are like shadows, darkening children's
>   days with fears of unknown calamities.
> Other beliefs are like the sunshine, blessing children
>   with the warmth of happiness . . .
> Some beliefs are like blinders, shutting off the power
>   to choose one's own direction.
> Other beliefs are like gateways opening up wide vistas
>   for exploration . . .
> Some beliefs are rigid, like the body of death, impotent
>   in a changing world.
> Other beliefs are pliable, like the young sapling, ever
>   growing with the upward thrust of life.
>   (*Today's Children and Yesterday's Heritage* p. 14.)

Parents, teachers, churches—all hinder the growth of children whenever indoctrination is put ahead of guidance. All the potentialities of the child can be evoked in due season under intelligent love and non-coercive attitudes. Parents and teachers should count it a privilege to walk with their children, shaping and reshaping their own beliefs and transcending them, as a snake sloughs off its outworn skin. It is true that each must learn to walk for himself, but persons can also learn the joy of walking together.

It is supreme wisdom to help our children realize that in life each must learn to see things for himself. When parents find their children echoing the adult stupidities picked up on the school playground from other children whose parents have indoctrinated them, they can say to them, "But you can see as well as anybody". A child can be guided into the pathway of intelligent questioning and away from dogmatic credulity. If "the priesthood of all believers" has any significance, it means that *in fundamentals* there is nothing the other person can do for one which one cannot do better for himself.

He who learns to grow, question, learn *in the present*— what someone has termed the intersection of time and eternity —knows inwardly the meaning of the phrase, "God is God of the living, not of the dead".

Protestantism also needs to reject the psychologically unsound and antiquated distinction between "sacred" and "profane", the "religious" and the "secular". This rejection, implicit in the Protestant principle, is too rarely made explicit. "Secularism" comes under attack again and again by all speakers or preachers hard up for sermon material and a whipping boy. What is "secularism" if not one way in which modern man makes a partial and relatively superficial response to the life process when he could be making a profounder, whole-natured response? And what is "religion" (or nonsecularism) but another partial, fragmentary response to the mystery of being, often just as one-sided as "secularism" because based on the same dualistic assumptions?

Are the churches any freer of superficiality and fragmentation than most other institutions? It was a devout Christian, John Oman, who wrote not long ago that the church is cursed with three "finalities"—fixed organizations, fixed ideals and fixed theologies. He added, "But as nothing is so bad as bad religion, just because religion is the most vital of all realities, so nothing in it may be more oppressive than a rule of the saints which is the perversion of God's real rule. Let us remind ourselves again that the chief cause of the Crucifixion was what regarded itself as a rule of the saints, and also that the Cross is a victory over this kind of rule above all". *(Honest Religion, p. 125).*

If we want to use the words "religious" and "secular" solely in a qualitative sense and without any institutional implications in principle, then we can say that the difference is solely one of depth—depth of intention and depth of seeing. Protestants need to learn how to open their eyes wider in order to see. Did not Walt Whitman see profoundly when he wrote:

> We consider bibles and religions divine—I do not say
> they are not divine;
> I say they have grown out of you, and may grow out of
> you still;
> It is not they who give the life—it is you who give the
> life;
> Leaves are not more shed from the trees, or trees from
> the earth, than they are shed out of you.
> ("Carol of Occupations," in *Leaves of Grass*.)

SUGGESTIONS FOR FURTHER READING

JOHN OMAN, *Honest Religion* (Cambridge and New York, 1941).
SOPHIA FAHS, *Today's Children and Yesterday's Heritage* (Boston, 1952).
W. E. GARRISON, *A Protestant Manifesto* (Nashville, 1952).
PAUL TILLICH, *The Protestant Era* (Chicago, 1948).

BEYOND PROTESTANTISM

By

Vergilius Ferm

BEYOND PROTESTANTISM

VERGILIUS FERM

THE TERM "Protestant" carries two meanings. It stems from the Latin *protestor* which, in turn, derives from *pro* meaning "on behalf of", "forth" or "openly" and *testor* meaning "witness to" or "being a witness". Thus, a Protestant is a bearer of witness *on behalf of* something. This usage dates back into the early centuries of Catholicism. The second meaning is also ancient. A *protestor* connotes an open and avowed dissent from some declaration or action. A Protestant, in this sense, is one who openly stands up *against* something, unwilling to accede or give approval. The first meaning which is positive in affirmation is undoubtedly the basic sense of the word. The second meaning which is negative always implies or connotes that which is unacceptable and opposed. According to the first meaning, anyone, Roman Catholic or non-Roman Catholic, is a Protestant. In the second meaning, a Protestant specifically is one who proclaims disagreement with certain declarations of the Roman Catholic ideas or practices.

In the second sense of the term Protestants were those who challenged Roman orthodoxy and polity before, during and after the sixteenth century Reformation. More particularly, the term was definitely applied to certain followers of Luther in Germany, some princes and representatives of free cities who, as a minority group, in 1529, declared their violent opposition to the majority decision at the second Diet of Spires (Speyer). The protests of the German Lutherans involved a resolution of the Diet to reject a previous declaration of the first Diet (1526) which had allowed each state to adopt the faith of its prince and thus permit religious divisions of Germany. The Lutherans protested against this reversal of position with the famous declaration of religious freedom: "In matters concerning God's honor and the salvation of souls each one must for himself stand before God and give account." The protest was issued as a document of appeal to a larger German assembly with a declaration of loyalty to the decisions of the earlier Diet. The term "Protestant" dates from this occasion—a term of specific dissension.

Like many terms in which the original specific meaning attached to specific circumstances is absorbed by a larger connotation, the term "Protestant" came to be applied to all those who dissented from the mother church, be they Lutherans in Germany or Reformed groups in France (Huguenots) and Switzerland—and, by extension, the dissenters of whatever group or sect or of whatever country whose history lies rooted in the sixteenth century period of the religious Reformation.

From the meaning of the term itself, then, a Protestant is both a dissenter and an affirmer: a dissenter from certain views and practices of Catholicism and a declarer of his own positive faith. Historically Protestantism has been just that: negative and positive, with now one emphasis and now another, but essentially both.

The "protests" of Protestants, historically, have been many. Originally there was a defiance of the practice known as indulgences by which those of the Catholic faith were permitted to work out penances imposed by the priest and shorten the journey to ultimate salvation. This was Martin Luther's initial protest as a Catholic. The abuses in the practice which lay in the circumvention of real sorrow for sins led to his emphasis upon justification by faith alone, without merit, in man's attainment of unity with God. Emphasis upon God's grace and the minimization of man's work or ethical conduct as merit lay at the heart of the teaching of all the great sixteenth century reformers. Man's utter incompetence and God's special dispensation of favor toward him became the awakened Protestant gospel. It was good news to realize that man's responsibility was minor compared with God's generosity. This led to the belief—based upon man's utter sinfulness and God's overwhelming grace to pardon and to forget because of the full merits offered by his Son in man's place—that those who benefit are "elected". Predestination was taught by the three major reformers, Luther, Zwingli and Calvin, the latter with great emphasis.

To protest against one doctrine and practice—that of indulgences—involved the graver charge against authority since the practice had the holy sanction of the head of the church. Logically and swiftly Luther was moving head on against a mighty ecclesiastical imperialism. All this became serious when forces rallied around him and so he and the early Protestants were hailed before church councils, excommunicated (in the case of Luther) and provinces of rebellious princes put under the ban. A Protestant, then, was marked as one who set himself against a *complete* allegiance to the church as represented by its chief spokesmen, the priest, the bishop and the pope. A higher authority than that of the church itself was substituted with enthusiastic allegiance on the part of the protestors. The Bible—the whole of it—soon took over as the sole arbitrator of religious doctrines and practices and on the correct interpretation of it Protestants contended with each other. This was the day before our present knowledge of the Scriptures (of its various literary forms, authorships, language, style) although Luther was one of the first to perceive the implications of the problems of original texts and translations and the necessity to discriminate the various degrees of worth of passages and even of some of its canonical books. The Bible—not the pope, nor the church, nor the priest, nor certain selections (pericopes) of Scripture—interpreted first-hand by lay-readers (the "open" Bible) became the absolute norm, higher than any council, creed, tradition, practice or even man's best opinion.

As is natural in the case of religious reformers moving out of a long tradition, there developed the conviction that the new reform was but a return to the primitive purity of view and practice. Many reformers felt this with deep conviction.

Some looked to Paul as the primitive expositor of the faith (*e.g.,* Luther); some saw in the Old Testament the compass by which to direct their course (as did the Calvinists in the case of the model city of Geneva patterned after a holy Israel); some saw in the manner of ordinances (baptism, the Lord's Supper, feet washing), of puritanical living (codes of conduct) the sure sign of such a return to a primitive and true church. Later, some saw a complete divorcement of the church as a divine institution from the state as a secular institution the mark of primitivism or the mark of the essential Christian way (*e.g.,* the Baptists). The invisible church (emphasized by Augustine) became for the major Protestant reformers the real church of Christ; the visible church, so many thought, had become too involved in Roman institutionalism with its forms of privileged hierarchy to go on without reform in polity. Some saw in a form of government, such as a ruling elder (Presbyterianism) or an official bishop (Episcopalianism) the conception of true polity according to primitivism. All were agreed that whatever differences Protestants may develop such practices or beliefs must be made secure in the primitive practices of the revealed Word of God. That differences continued to divide Protestants was not regarded as surprising since each difference rested upon a deep conviction that it was Scripturally grounded and thus had the blessing of God ultimately. All were agreed that the Scriptures had been superseded by inroads of ecclesiastical interpretation and practice not in conformity with the Scriptures themselves. This was a major protest of the early Protestants on which they agreed in principle although they differed in both interpretations of ideas and practices permitted by the Scriptures. A layman can understand "God's Word" and needs not a priest to interpret it for him—a claim which persisted in theory among the Protestants but which was surrendered in practice by the formation of Protestant catechisms, creeds, symbols and confessional standards.

It must not be forgotten that the early Protestants were

Catholics. The Reformation principles were revolutionary in terms of a long tradition and liberal to the point of modernity. But for all that, the Protestant Reformation was fundamentally conservative. To a large degree it was Catholicism reformed, the mother spoken up to but not altogether disowned. In England this was particularly true and continues to be true in the established church. The Anglican Church, by and large, prefers to be called Catholic rather than Protestant. Among Lutherans Catholicism persisted conspicuously in the continuation of forms of Catholic worship (*e.g.,* liturgies and the idea and practice of a revised mass). A Lutheran insists upon a "real presence" in the sacrament of the altar and "regeneration" in baptism with emphasis upon sacramental grace. The harsh manner of Presbyterian polity in matters of discipline in the church, questions of doctrinal subscription and over-all policy and the harsh legalism of inherited Calvinism, are vestiges of the mother church. Calvinistic Puritanism was as intolerant as the old mother had been toward any who might wander too far from theological and other fences. Presbyterianism was not alone in such matters. Presbyterianism, however, exerted an enormous influence among other dissenting groups such as the Congregational, the Baptist and even among some Methodists (whose own rigors were more in protest against Episcopalian religious laxities). Calvinism has carried on many of the features of Roman Catholicism. The pattern of the Protestants was essentially Catholic in spite of the inroads of liberalism.

The sacramental emphasis in Protestantism is also a part of this heritage—and acknowledged by Protestants as such. Although dropping five of the Catholic sacraments as sacraments or especial grace conferring ordinances (confirmation, marriage, ordination, penance and extreme unction) Protestants were certain that two of the traditional number were primitive in practice and significance (baptism and the Lord's Supper). Roman Catholicism was acknowledged right on this point of two sacraments (though having five more) although their developed theories about the sacraments were regarded as un-scriptural, particularly the Lord's Supper. Anglican Protestants (those of the so-called "high church") kept the seven, calling two of them "sacraments of the gospel" and the remaining five "sacramentalia".

It follows that Protestants gave to other of their religious heritages an emphasis of their own. Prayers for pardon, for example, were stressed as immediate and self-sufficient trans-actions between the believer and his God in need of no special medium of priest or intercessory. Catholics, of course, believed in individuals' prayers for pardon but they had, in the eyes of the Protestants, attached too much significance to the role of the priesthood in the certainties of absolution. The priest by reason of his holy and sacramental ordination assumed the privileged status of pronouncing absolution and assurance of forgiveness whereas the Protestant considered the *promises* of Christ himself as sufficient for such absolution and assurance (although a minister as a servant may announce the fact). Penitence for the Protestant is an inner state of the sensitive spirit wherein contrition for sin of itself needs no set of reme-dial acts imposed by a priest. For the Catholic penitence be-comes involved in penance, a working out of penalties assigned by the priest. Penance came to be involved in private confes-sion to a priest and the rendering of satisfactions which, if not redeemed, required a continued state of purgatory where ac-cumulated punishments are to be worked out.

Again, the church for the Protestant is a means toward an end and not itself an end. Both Calvin and Zwingli taught that those outside the church may be saved if God so willed. Catholics emphasize the necessity of the church in matters of salvation. For the Catholic the church is invisible-visible and a tangible thing. For the Protestant the real church is invisible and only secondarily visible. The minister is ordained to holy profession in the Protestant view, set aside by consecration (laying on of hands). For the Catholic the act of consecration confers a special miracle of grace (sacramental) and gives certain privileges and rights to its priests which are unique and which stand higher than any secular powers. For the Protestant each believer is his own priest, serving his fellowmen and being served by them on the level of a common Christian fraternity. All honorable work is a vocation (or call) equally high in the sight of the Lord to the Protestant; for the Catholic a priest enjoys a sacramentally privileged role in Christ's kingdom, holding office which, divinely instituted, is above any other in the economy of man. For both groups a minister or priest is a mediator; but for the Catholic the priest is a mediator with special inherent ecclesiastical and ambassadorial powers. Thus, the chief priest (the pope) is held to be beyond question in matters of faith and morals by reason of his highest order. For Protestants the emphasis is upon the dignity of laymen, the humblest of believers, who possess inherent rights and privileges by reason of their discipleship with Christ. A Protestant may dispense with the official priest at no peril to his salvation, though he need not dispense with the official ministry provided its prerogatives are regarded as functional rather than inherently and especially privileged. Protestants, theoretically if not always practically, look across their borders to Catholics believing that Christians are not confined to one church or to one system of theology and ecclesiastical polity. Catholics believe, both theoretically and practically, that there is but one pattern of religious truth and that departure on the part of anyone (including a Protestant) from this essential pattern (defined by their councils) is a risk too great to undertake in the matter of one's ultimate salvation.

Protestant worship characteristically is congregation-centered. As contrasted with Catholic forms, worshippers share in active participation. A Roman Catholic priest performs at the altar vicariously for his congregation and they share reverently by watching and listening and answering the signals from the altar. The whole Catholic service is centered upon submission, and, in the high mass, to a reverent gaze upon the dramatic renewal of the supreme Sacrifice at the altar, a *fait accompli*.

The music is ancient and classic and requires professional performance in the niceties of ritual. For Protestants, singing
and responsive readings are more informally ordered and there
is less the feeling that a dramatic performance goes on up
front. Preaching came in with full emphasis among the early
Protestant leaders and remains a characteristic feature of the
Protestant service. It is an appeal for active response to those
in the pews rather than a formal announcement to them or
something done in their behalf.

This people-centered emphasis, however, does not always
obtain in all Protestant churches. There are those liturgical
churches which revert to Catholic practices; and there are
those non-liturgical churches which have revived complicated
liturgies, formal and professional music, which appeal to
aesthetic enjoyment rather than to the strictly religious motiva-
tion. Wherever preaching takes a secondary place in Protestant
practice such practice is a forfeiture of the very essence of
original Protestantism. Luther was a preacher of power and
persuasion. Zwingli stood in the pulpit for long hours ex-
pounding verses of Scripture. Calvin was strong in his pulpit
appealing as he did to the intelligentsia of his day by orderly
exposition and logical persuasion. The Protestant Reformation was a people's movement against vested interests and
against vicarious expressions of religion. Things were happen-
ing inside of people. The Reformation came not from inside
the machinery of the ancient institution. To wait upon a
preacher to bear witness of what the Scriptures really had to
say was as great an event in that early day as was to wait for
the postman to bring the news of the day or, in our own time,
to listen to a professional commentator of the latest releases
over the radio. The Scriptures were being unfolded as never
before in the vernacular of the day with astounding freshness,
stimulating curiosity and interest. The church was finding
something to say to the people which seemed altogether new
to them though the source was as old as the long centuries.
The preachers were the bearers of these tidings and were less

the priests who had been ministering before ancient altars. The pulpit became an important spot on the stage. And, as time went on, this new focus changed even the architecture of the churches so that the word spoken might be better heard by the participating congregation. In many Protestant churches the pulpit even supplanted the altar. All through Protestant history ministers were expected to speak and to have something stirring to say rather than merely to perform the routine of an ancient ceremony. One is tempted to ask: has this preaching ministry in current Protestantism become a lost art in the mazes of complicated formal programs of worship and in the compression of curtailed time?

* * * * * *

In the history of Christianity Protestantism is but a chapter. It is important to realize this point. Many Protestants take the view of their Protestant faith much like the Catholics theirs: they tend to think of it *as such* as something fixed and final. Protestantism like Catholicism on such a view becomes an end and not a means, the whole story and not a chapter in the larger account of Christianity.

Can it be that there are other chapters *beyond* Protestantism?

One is here reminded of an analogy. Education is both an informing and a transforming process. The informing portion is one of indoctrination, of passing on the accepted mores, knowledge and wisdom of the past to be carried on into the future. This is to make disciples: learners from elders. But there is the other side to education. The very word *educare* suggests *leading out of* or taking out of a person something that he himself has to contribute so that it is a process of his own digestion and his own transformation of what he learns from his teachers and *from himself*. An educated person thus (in both meanings) is one who learns from the treasures offered by his teachers and the past but who at the same time contributes something of himself and of the contemporary situation to what he learns.

Historic Protestantism was similar to this two-fold meaning of education—but only to a degree. It took over much from its past and, at the same time, its early leaders gave something of themselves to it which transformed the heritage into something fresh and prophetic and new. In the first sense it remained a *Catholic* Protestantism; in the second sense it became a *Protestant* Protestantism.

The many children of Protestantism have gone on in a similar two-fold direction: those whose Protestantism, looking back to what the early Protestants taught and believed, has set forth a more or less closed system made normative in the writings (and confessional affirmations) of an earlier Protestant day. The current revival of the movement known as neo-orthodoxy in theological circles is just this *type* of Protestantism: it is a Protestantism that is traditional in emphasis, a return to the essential patterns of sixteenth century thought (with modifications, *e.g.,* of inherited views of the Scriptures, etc.). "Let us re-read Luther and let us try to understand Calvin and let the great principles underlying Calvin's *Institutes* once more come to the light of our way"—so they seem to say. Conservative Protestantism of our day—in the broad sense of that term—is a revival of a *Catholic* Protestantism taken to be genuine and the only kind worthy of the name.

The other direction in which Protestants have gone—and by far this is the party of the minority—has been in transforming the heritage into something *beyond* it. This *Protestant* Protestantism looks back upon original forms as but a chapter in the whole history of Christianity, a chapter of achievement, indeed, as compared to other chapters—but still only a chapter. The story of Christianity is not yet finished and there are new scenes to come up and new visions to behold. This new direction may be as transforming of Protestantism as was Protestantism, in certain of its features, in its Catholic beginnings. In the analogy of education, the child may look back with appreciation to what he has learned but he himself is now taking over, writing his own story according to what he himself finds important for his own day and ready to make his own protests and affirmations even though he must part company with his revered teachers.

We have, then, two kinds of Protestants: the *Catholic* Protestants (doing very much the same as their Catholic competitors), conservative, looking back to the Confessions of the church, quoting the fathers, speaking of the Scriptures much in the same normative way as the fathers, emphasizing doctrines which the fathers underlined (*e.g.,* the utter sinfulness of man, the mind of man standing over against the will of God, salvation from a world alien to God, a Chalcedonian Christology, and the like) and, of course, making much of the forms of organization which have persisted through more than four centuries (elders, bishops)—all the while claiming to be Scriptural and therefore securely grounded. These Protestants are found for the most part in conventional churches; they meet in annual conventions under the laws of their ecclesiastical governments; their ministers preach sermons acceptable to their tradition; their Seminary professors are bound more or less to the oaths of office of their church in which there shall be no too great departure from standards already set; and their young ministers come out much as priests to carry on "the sound doctrine" of their church. Denominational publishing houses are careful to scan manuscripts since there must be the *imprimatur* of church boards; foreign missionaries must be subject to foreign boards which in turn must be subject to the ecclesiastical disciplines. Thus the wheels turn smoothly—unless, perchance, here and there, some recalcitrant individual bobs up to stir dust in the oil. But such recalcitrants are taken care of either by lack of promotion, demotion, by being ignored or sent to out-of-the-way parishes or else brought to the ecclesiastical carpet for authoritative chastisement and perhaps expulsion. The machinery of the *Catholic* Protestant church has been grinding as exultantly and pontifically as anything in historic Catholicism. In many places this is not just history; it is still contemporary,

The other group has found itself either in the minority within the Protestant church, going its way quietly and unofficially, or else it has set up an organized group which the larger conventional churches officially ignore. In the ecumenical Protestant movement, for example, the Unitarians and the Universalists and others have not counted. Their Protestantism is perhaps too Protestant for other Protestants. They are not Catholic enough: too informal, too unmanageable, too individualistic, too heretical on certain doctrines (for example, Trinity, soteriology, Christology, etc.). But they, too, are Protestant in spirit and even in heritage.

In and out of the pews of many churches today we find the latter group, the *Protestant* Protestants, growing in number and finding their own conventional churches somewhat unrealistic. The minds of their conventionally trained ministers seem set apart from them: a chasm that is strange. There is a lack of reality-feeling for the traditional way of presenting religion, even the Protestant faith. There is a vague feeling after something constructive that is reconstructive. From many conventional Protestant pulpits the message does not yield the note of contemporaneity. The conventional phrases are there and they are respected. But their meaning is not quite realistic. A gulf is growing between the pulpit and the pew. In some churches the chasm is being bridged by an attempt to appeal to a universal sense of beauty: music, architecture, ritual, robed choirs. And to a significant degree all this works. But there still remains an appetite that is not being satisfied, an emptiness that has not been filled. Such lay Protestants who sense this gap are turning to the psychiatrists (in growing numbers), to inspiring magazines called Digests, to syndicated columns written by physicians who now know that psychosomatic medicine is important, to a general groping in their thinking and reading, listening to choice voices on the Sunday radio (disappointed, of course, with the Sunday howlings of religious superficialities). Those who are less discriminate follow the way of the cults which, in turn, grow by leaps and bounds.

But let us remember that Protestant beginnings were among men learned in the profession. Luther was a college professor; Zwingli a classical humanist; Calvin, both a humanist and a university trained mind in law and theology. This made them not better than anyone else; but it gave them a sense of mission. The enlightened people were not to be shunted aside in favor of some cheap sentimental religious approach or by restating old Protestant slogans. The head and reason may have its difficulties but the appeal was not against reason so much as it was something that led reason into greater adventures than the prison-house of inherited scholasticism. Indeed, Luther was given to extreme statements in pitting faith against reason; but he himself was no mean thinker (although unsystematic) when it came to rationalize his religion. Calvin and Zwingli never overthrew their humanistic culture even though they got bogged down by their predestinarian views. It was their logic and their reason that bogged them down, particularly the former.

Protestantism moved away from classical humanism. Erasmus unfortunately broke with Luther as did Luther with Erasmus. It was a tragic event in consequence. But there were other humanists who moved in to take part even though their humanism was not of the same cloth. Melanchthon, Luther's right-hand man, never forgot his humanism. Arminianism and Methodism had its form of humanism which made man important in the drama of salvation, at least by making him responsible for the outcome by his rejection or acceptance of the proferred grace.

Protestantism today, however, may have to move much further than ever before anticipated. The fully emancipated mind which is of the essence of *Protestant* Protestantism has before it no limits of restrictions except the limitations of hard-won truth and growing and consecrated experience. This phase in the chapter of the history of Christianity has, of course, not come fully to its own but indications of its initial stirrings are becoming more and more explicit. It will be a chapter which may well be written larger than ever before—one that may be called "Beyond Protestantism" standing upon the shoulders of the Protestant fathers but seeing visions unimagined by them.

* * * * * *

The two areas of great transformation will come both in thought and organization, in theology and polity. The larger organizational expressions will be those of unity amidst variety, not unity in conformity. It will be in terms of the full realization of differences in the cultures of men, of backgrounds and of human personalities. No existing ecumenical organizations shall contain it since it is beyond the patterns of present formal organizations. It will move in the direction of programs of social efforts where those of other ethnic faiths will meet those of the Christian stream to work out common bases of understanding rather than devices for mutual conversions. Each tree has its own roots but the common foliage of many trees may by their intertwined branches form a unity in spite of their several varieties.

On the theological side the new moulds will probably be so different that a question may be raised as to their connection with historic Protestantism. The *beyond* will not be verbal; it will be radical.

What shall transpire will be analogous to what has been transpiring in other areas of human inquiry wherever these have really been free to inquire. No human progress can ever come without liberated minds, minds really emancipated from the clutches of organizational and traditional mandates. We have today a physics that is as new and revolutionary as the Newtonian was in relation to Aristotelian science. We have today gropings in the fields of medicine and biology which are as revolutionary as the beginnings of modern medicine were to medieval magic. We have today technologies that have completely altered the way of everyday life so that were the sixteenth century Reformers alive they would have to be almost altogether reconditioned to get on in the world. We have today so much transforming information about our Scriptures, the Scriptures of other peoples, of ancient languages, of social origins, of the influence of psychological factors upon beliefs and practices, that a new note is being sounded in liberal religious thinking. We have today a new economic way of life that is dawning upon us due to the rapid intercommunication and exchange which will make our yesteryears seem almost medieval and provincial. Theology alone, of all disciplines, seems to be the last to come up for muster in the modern parade. It still wears old clothes, sings ancient and unrealistic poetry (as witness the conventional hymnals), uses out-worn phrases. This is, of course, because theology is so closely woven to religion which, in turn, is conservative touching the sentimental phases of life. Men give up their gods and goddesses unwillingly since they fear their wrath and hesitate to play fast and loose with matters of ultimate destiny. Religious ways, religious institutions, are rooted deep in feelings. The head may see but the emotions motivate. We gladly light our homes by electricity when we wish to read; but we still prefer candles on our birthdays and anniversaries.

Does this mean that the teachings of Christ are outmoded or that God has been deceiving the children of men? By no means. It signifies only that we may have trusted too much other men's theories about Christ and about a plan of salvation, their ideas of "who are of the elect".

Can theology remain unaffected by all such revolutionary changes of our current culture? If so, this will be something new in history! Theology has always been affected by factors outside of itself. Paul's theology was influenced by Jewish and Hellenic culture. Augustine's thought shows the influence of current philosophy (Neoplatonism) and the decaying civilization of his day. Anselm's theology bursts with feudalistic ideas and practices. Luther's theology reveals not only a turbulent soul but the social turmoils of a growing German self-con-

sciousness. Calvin showed the defense mechanism of self-pre-
servation by his own rigorous application of conceptions of
law, of rule, of order in God's kingdom where the Will of
God is absolute—in a day of fierce persecutions and inroads
upon his work in Geneva. Neo-orthodoxy today is a reflection
of the pessimisms attending World Wars. Theology never
stands in a social vacuum. When it is alive it reflects its time;
otherwise it is an anachronism and, by such token, merely
formal.

This mid-century will probably go down in history as one of
the major bends in the human road. There is no longer a virtue
in being simply "a Protestant" as such. Virtue consists in having some of the courage of our Protestant fathers to express
prophetically and realistically what lies in developing human
needs and in the changing order of things.

* * * * * *

Beyond Protestantism will imply:

A re-evaluation of the mind of Christ as something that is
greater than any single tradition or church or inherited theology. It will imply a re-emphasis upon values which cut across
all cultures, all peoples. For values which have the mark of
the eternal are not imprisoned by one set or pattern of ideas,
one group of creeds, by one church institution. The mind of
Christ is wider than the reaches of a single course of history:
it is something that all men everywhere may respond to not because of the saying of some Scripture but because of the universal responses to that mind in the hearts of men everywhere.

A re-evaluation of the Scriptures will show that many if not
all of its *essential* teachings find parallels in other great cultures. The brotherhood of man, the sonship of men under one
living Spirit, the trustworthiness of the best ideals of sacrifice,
service and the outreaching of the human spirit and feeling
that there is in this world a Spirit that touches the best in all
sons of men—these are universal experiences which cannot be
copyrighted at one place or in a single book or verse. The

Scriptures of other civilizations belong with those of our own tradition revealing the pilgrimage of man toward the same fundamental ends of life, now showing at one place in better light and now showing in less light. We shall not continue to believe that this Spirit is confined to our own group of elect (an idea inherited from Judaism and revived and emphasized in Catholicism and renewed in *Catholic* Protestantism). We shall not look down upon others as having been misled by some ugly Devil into the ways of untruth; but rather to sense the same Spirit at work because it is one world and all men equally share in the birthright of sons of the same God.

A re-evaluation of the doctrines of inherited Protestantism will show their truth to lie in human experience rather than in the statement of some council or hallowed tradition. The vicarious sacrifice of Christ is a law of life and is vindicated as an eternal truth in the very nature of life at its best. Atonement is a universal experience brilliantly dramatized at Golgotha. Justification by faith is not a mere Protestant conception but is the way of all true faith. When one trusts, one's trust brings about a fulfillment of purpose not otherwise possible. This is not an isolated dogma; it is a living truth. The priesthood of all believers is true in that in so far as people share in some joy or some sorrow sympathetically they minister to one another without the need of some official third party. In any genuine society all share equally the burdens and the victories; and the lines between men fade in the degree that they share.

When we read that the true church is invisible we know how true this is since all the great mutual experiences are fundamentally beyond the show of statistics or numbers or quantities. The real church is a quality rather than a quantity. In this it becomes the kingdom of God. That fruits issue from faith is a commonplace; for men's actions reveal their fundamental commitments. The Sonship of Christ to God is a symbol which has meaning far exceeding the analogy of the Jewish family. It implies the relationship that where the mind of Christ is there is genuine family relationship of belonging to the Divinity of Life. That the historic Christ possessed this relation is the essential meaning of Sonship.

The emancipation of the individual and the freedom of his own conscience are doctrines made holy in the whole struggle of mankind, be it East or West, and is a fundamental law of life in the principle of individuality all through nature. The attempt to crush this is to toy with the laws of nature. The sinfulness of man is acknowledged by most men in their conscious mistakes, their ignorance, their finiteness, their limitations, their undue self-assertiveness. But such sinfulness is not a curse but a fact of all creatureliness. It does not imply that men shall remain forever under some curse or be condemned to a status alien to God for which there is no solution other than a providential deal set up by some eternal decree; rather, men shall learn to profit by constant struggle with themselves and the forces which seem to make all life a struggle and thus the creation of virtues. This struggle need not be considered lonely even though it does at times—even for the Man of Sorrows it did seem so at his dramatic moment in Gethsemane. There are resources in the world and such resources are the gifts of Divine grace.

The great affirmation of historic Protestantism, the emphasis upon the grace of God, is a doctrine not learned from books but an experience of everyday life. Life itself is a gracious gift. For we came into this world not by reason of our own efforts, nor do we live altogether healthily by what we do. The whole transaction of life itself is the miracle of grace, a free gift bestowed for which we remain always in debt of utter gratitude and responsive appreciation. A man may by his own efforts achieve many things; but underlying the very essence of life is the grace of the creative power that makes such efforts possible and worthy and ultimately significant. One does not have to be a Protestant or a Catholic to believe this. That Christ exemplifies or manifests God's grace is not to be doubted; for Christ is also the Son of Man and man can well understand the fundamental and universal truth involved.

Revelation is not a fixed but a growing experience as it always has been—from ancient times to the present. Man's discoveries of the mysteries of life, of values, of nature, are, from the side of Deity, revelations of what is existentially real. Some discoveries may be more significant than others. We shall not for one moment deny the great discoveries of our own tradition nor shall we deny to others that they too, in their own way, have made discoveries of significance. There are not many Gods. There is One God. And God is not a tribal deity but a Universal Spirit brooding upon the hearts of men everywhere. It is man who makes artificial divisions. It is one of his major sins. The scandal of denominational arrogances is pitifully small in comparison with the arrogances of Christians toward others of alien faiths or the arrogances of other religious people toward Christians.

Evils in the world are not of one kind; there are some that belong to the weather and to the soil; there are some that belong to the sheer accidents of conflicting forces beyond man's control; there are some which are errors of judgment; and there are still others that are malicious and planned behavior, the inhumanity of man to man. But evils may be transmuted into goods and these, in turn, may be re-transmuted into other evils. Goods and evils are to be measured in terms of direction. In themselves they are always related to contexts. To follow after the best, under Divine beneficence, is the good-in-direction; to follow after the worse is the bad-in-direction. We are not to be saved from evil; but we are to be saved from going in a direction which makes evil our God (the devil). We are not to be saved out of this world; we are to be saved to something that is better in it. No man is expected to be perfect. "Be ye perfect" is an injunction to set the sights. To aspire to perfection means to set the course, not to look longingly for a state of equanimity. Hell there is when there is no sense of direction or where the direction makes for our own ultimate nihility and renders impossible our turning around (our redemption).

Personal immortality there is, not because of some saying in Scripture nor because of some physical demonstration but because there is a Spirit which conserves personal values as worthy of persistence and the response of our better selves in the unquenchable hope that such values may never perish. One believes in a personal immortality much as one believes that there will be an awakening in a tomorrow's day after having forgotten for a while in the silence of sleep. We act upon these recurrent eventualities not as proofs but as a common-place trust in the trustworthiness of life itself to mend and recharge its inherent vitalities.

Redemption means to be brought back into favor where that favor seems to have been lost sight of. Man as a creature needs redemption not once-for-all but as a continual renewal. This, too, is a law of life. Forgiveness is a necessity of living, not a luxury. For without it the mistakes we make for ourselves and toward others make us permanent slaves to them. Forgiveness is the step forward after we have been walking backward.

. . . So the pattern takes shape. Is this Protestantism? Is this Christianity? The Catholic answer both in Catholicism and *Catholic* Protestantism may be a rude "No". The Protestant answer if it is a *Protestant* Protestantism is "Yes" for the reason that the essentials remain although the theology and soteriology may be clothed in brand new garments. It is *beyond* Protestantism in that the pattern does not conform to a traditional Protestantism nor does it worship any label. *Beyond* means that labels and phrases may become a form of idolatry wherever they stand in the way for a more adequate expression of deeper truths and of more pressing needs.

Thinking people of the Christian heritage today really care little whether one is a Lutheran or Reformed or Presbyterian. The labels mean less and less for the simple reason that something else means more and more. This is what is meant by "beyond"—something more significant than merely being a Protestant. It is being a Christian in a larger sense—much larger than envisaged by those of the sixteenth and following centuries in the tradition. It is not parting company with the heritage completely; it is transforming and transmuting that heritage to the demands of our day. It may well be (as some may wish to call it) a new religion. But it is a new religion with roots that reach back, however vaguely, through many centuries in time and finds accord with human hearts across many cultures. We only need now to make bold to affirm it more openly in a new Reformation *beyond* Protestantism.

SUGGESTIONS FOR FURTHER READING

GAIUS GLENN ATKINS, *Resources for Living* (New York, 1938).

ROBERT O. BALLOU (editor), *The Bible of the World* (New York, 1939).

PAUL BLANSHARD, *American Freedom and Catholic Power* (Boston, 1949).

EDGAR S. BRIGHTMAN, *The Spiritual Life* (New York and Nashville, 1942).

FRED I. CAIRNS, *Progress is Unorthodox* (Boston, 1950).

RUTH CRANSTON, *World Faith* (The Story of the Religions of the United Nations) (New York, 1949).

VERGILIUS FERM, *What Can We Believe?* (New York, 1948).

———, (editor), *Religion in the Twentieth Century* (New York, 1948).

———, *A Protestant Dictionary* (New York, 1951).

———, (editor), *The American Church* (New York, 1953).

JAMES GORDON GILKEY, *A Faith to Affirm* (New York, 1940).

EDGAR J. GOODSPEED, *Christianity Goes to Press* (New York, 1940).

CONRAD H. MOEHLMAN, *The Wall of Separation between Church and State* (Boston, 1951).

FLOYD H. ROSS, *Addressed to Christians*: Isolationism vs. World Community (New York, 1950).

HENRY N. WIEMAN, *Methods of Private Religious Living* (New York, 1929).

INDEX

[231]

INDEX

INDEX

INDEX

INDEX

INDEX